C000137307

100 INSPIRA

BUILD YOUR RESILIENCE

Jo Banks

Jo Banks

First Edition: January 2021

Copyright © 2021 - Jo Banks

Published by What Next? Media – info@whatnextconsultancy.co.uk

Jo Banks

For Sharon

Thanks for always being there; for your continuous, never-ending support, loyalty and belief in me. For reminding me who I am and what I'm capable of, even when I fail to see it for myself. x

"

Thoughts Become Things: Change Your Thoughts, Change Your World

Jo Banks

Content

Jo Banks

Foreword

Jo Banks

Foreword

Welcome to my eighth book – 100 Motivational Moments. I can't believe that I'm on book eight already. It's been a strange old journey, but an interesting one!

100 MM follows on from my first book, *'Thoughts Become Things: Change Your Thoughts, Change Your World'*. It has evolved due to feedback from my coaching clients and readers, suggesting that it would be helpful to have a quick reference guide, providing inspiration and tips to help build and maintain resilience and positivity.

Our lives are so diverse and fast-paced with such an excessive amount of change, especially since COVID-19 hit us, that it's sometimes hard to stay positive and motivated. However, a well-timed piece of advice or a short positive reminder can make all the difference in moving us out of learnt helpless and into a position of power.

According to scientific research, more than genetics, more than intelligence, more than any other factor, it is how we think that determines whether we are resilient or not. Therefore, our thinking styles are of fundamental importance in this book.

With that in mind, I have specifically designed 100 MM to deliver an instant boost of inspiration for when you need it most. As with 'Thoughts', it's packed full of quick, easy to use ideas, tools and techniques specifically designed to encourage you to build and maintain your innate resilience and positivity.

As I have designed it to be a quick guide, I haven't gone into each topic in detail. However, everything I've included has been thoroughly researched and tested with thousands of my clients, delegates and readers.

How am I qualified to write 100 MM?

Since I set up my own business, What Next Consultancy (www.whatnextconsultancy.co.uk) in 2009, I have personally coached hundreds of people, with thousands having attended my leadership development courses and webinars. Previous to that, I worked for twenty years as a senior H.R. professional, where coaching and supporting staff at every level, from board directors to shop floor workers, was an integral part of my day to day job.

Working with so many people with such diverse backgrounds and problems would have meant I was worryingly unobservant had I not recognised specific patterns in thinking and behaviour that affect our ability to attain the lives we desire. It's these thoughts, emotions and behaviours that I'll be addressing throughout this book.

Over the years, I have developed a comprehensive toolkit based on principles taken from my formal training as a Master N.L.P. Practitioner (Neurolinguistic Programming), C.B.T. Therapist (Cognitive Behavioural Therapy), Executive Coach and E.F.T. Practitioner (Emotional Freedom Technique).

As well as incorporating the most powerful techniques from these practices, I have included ideas and principles gained from personally attending countless workshops, courses and seminars in the field of human potential. I make a point of reading/listening to at least two self-development or business-related books per month (having read well over 600 to date). I also have a new-found love of Podcasts which helps me stay up to date on the latest ideas and research on high-impact success principles.

The knowledge gained from such a wide variety of sources has significantly influenced my coaching and ability to influence and help create positive changes in others.

Jo Banks

I've tried and tested many 'self-help' tools and techniques both on myself and my clients throughout the years, and now have a substantial practical toolkit which I'm sharing with you in 100 MM. I have included nothing here that isn't easy to use and proven to produce long-lasting results repeatedly.

This stuff works!

Introduction

Jo Banks

Introduction

How to Use this Book

There are several ways to use this book:

1. Read it in its entirety.
2. Read a 'Moment' each morning or evening as part of your regular routine.
3. Dip in, choosing a page randomly whenever you need a blast of positivity or inspiration. It's likely that when you do this, the 'Moment' you hit upon will contain the information you most need to hear at that point.

I've purposely kept it smaller than my other books so that it doesn't take up too much space, making it easier to keep it with you by the side of your bed, on your desk, in your bag/pocket, etc. giving you instant access to a positivity boost whenever you need it.

As you read delve in, you may find that there is just one small thing that resonates with you, and that causes you to take action as a result. All significant change starts with the first thought. Any actions you take as a result of

17

Jo Banks

reading this book will be a course set in motion, positively affecting your life (and the lives of the people you interact with); that is my intention for you.

Repetition

You will notice that I have repeated some points throughout this book. That's because I consider them to be essential for you to understand, learn and put into practice. After all, *repetition is the mother of skill!*

Terminology

Below are explanations of some of the terminology I've used. You'll notice that I have cross-referenced back to this section where I think it's helpful.

- Neural Pathways

- Programming

- Learnt Behaviour

- Learnt Helplessness

- The Spiral Effect

- Reticular Activating System

- Internal vs External Focus

- N.E.T. – No Extra Time

Neural Pathways

A neural pathway is a brain connection that enables a signal to get sent from one region of the nervous system to another. When brain cells communicate frequently, the link between them strengthens and the messages travelling repeatedly, begin to transmit faster and faster.

When you have a thought or take some action for the first time, you create a neural pathway, albeit a light one. When you have the same thought or carry out the same action repeatedly, the link deepens. With enough repetition, they become automatic, i.e. you no longer have to think about them consciously; the thought or action becomes automatic.

To explain how neural pathways work, let's use the example of learning to drive. At first, it is hard to remember the correct sequence, e.g. mirror, signal, manoeuvre (that's because the neural pathway is light). However, the more you practise, the easier it becomes. After many hours of 'rehearsal', you stop thinking consciously about it, and because the pathway becomes so deep, driving is almost automatic.

This is an essential part of a healthy functioning brain; it is designed to pass frequently executed tasks form the conscious to the unconscious mind as quickly as possible. If it didn't work this way, we'd have to consciously think about everything we do, e.g. getting out of bed, cleaning our teeth, opening a door, etc.

However, problems can occur when the thought or behaviour that we've built a strong neural pathway for, is negative or unhelpful, as that too will become automatic.

Deepening neural pathways explains how we create habits, good or bad; the process is the same. For example, ex-smokers often reach for a cigarette even when they stopped smoking years before. The neural pathway associated with smoking will be so deep after years of repetition that the subconscious will automatically drive the behaviour without conscious thought.

Programming/Conditioning

As children, when we grow, we make sense of the world around us by unconsciously reviewing the information we receive through sight, sound, taste, smell by running it through our 'filters'.

Initially, we develop our filters (or programmes) in two ways; by copying our primary caregivers and trial and error. However, as we develop and become exposed to new ideas and stimuli throughout our lifetime, we can consciously choose to change unhelpful ones – the most challenging part is recognising that they *are* unhelpful in the first instance.

When we are young, our primary caregivers (mothers, fathers, grandparents, teachers, etc.) are a dominant influence on our thoughts and behaviours. We continuously watch what they say and react to certain people and situations and *subconsciously* copy them.

As children, we have no other references and are unknowingly *programmed or conditioned* by what we see, hear and feel going on around us. As the neural pathways deepen with practice, our reactions become 'learnt behaviours' that control how we react to similar situations and people throughout the rest of our lives (unless we *consciously* choose to think/behave differently).

Problems can occur when the people we 'model' as children have negative or unhelpful programming themselves; it's likely that they'll have received faulty programming in the very the same way.

'Faulty' or unhelpful conditioning can repeat for generations until someone finally makes a conscious decision to think, do or say something different.

If you've read my first book, 'Thoughts Become Things',

you'll know that I grew up in an incredibly pessimistic 'victim' type household. For the first 30 years or so of my life, I didn't realise there was any other way of being. I was so programmed by negativity, that it was all I knew. It never even occurred to me that there was an alternative.

I knew other people were 'different'; but to me, they just seemed to be blessed. Their lives appeared to be easy, uncomplicated, and they were happy. I thought that they must be lucky (at least that's what I got conditioned to believe) when my family and I were quite obviously not.

I can't remember exactly how I came across it, but I read Paul McKenna's excellent book, 'Change Your Life in 7 Days', and it did precisely that. It had such a profound impact on me that it changed absolutely everything, forever.

I started to devour everything I could find relating to self-development, how the brain works, how to be successful, and how to live a happy, healthy life by opening myself up to different experiences, people, situations, points of view, etc. I was able to see a whole new range of possibilities and options.

I started to tune into my thoughts consciously. Whenever I noticed any negativity, I actively changed it; each time, creating new neural pathways. With repetition, they deepened and, over time, my updated thoughts and reactions became automatic (replacing the old), allowing me to be far more productive, resourceful and successful.

Learnt Behaviour

As we become 'programmed', our reactions to certain people, situations and stimuli become automatic 'learnt behaviours'.   We learn most of our responses and thinking patterns up to the age of seven. After that age, the way the brain functions changes. Our subconscious brain searches for something comparable with each new scenario or experience and applies the same programmed/conditioned response.

To explain 'trial and error' (the other way we learn our reactions); think of a child who discovers that when they cry, they get comforted, and the problem gets taken away from them.   Because their actions produce a positive result, the unconscious mind will likely adopt that response to similar situations in the future.

However, as we learn most of our reactions up to the age of seven, this can be problematic in adulthood.   For example, I often coach female executives and businesswomen who cry when they become angry or frustrated.   That is typically a learnt behaviour that probably served them well as a child (i.e., when they got upset, someone picked them up, comforted them and solved the 'problem' for them), but it's no longer appropriate as an adult.

Interestingly, men rarely have this issue. As children, boys are typically told, 'boys don't cry', and as a result, they learn to bury their feelings. We know that mental health issues for men in their 20s, 30s and 40s are an increasing problem; 'learnt behaviour' from childhood is undoubtedly a contributing factor.

As adults, we can change unhelpful conditioning, but we have to be conscious of it, building and developing new neural pathways the replace the old. However, it isn't necessarily difficult. Often, when something no longer makes sense to the subconscious mind, it will automatically change with minimal conscious effort.

In summary, the saying, *'You can't teach an old dog new tricks'* isn't true at all! You most certainly can; by building new neural pathways to replace the outdated ones. As I said earlier, the most challenging part of changing is to recognise when you have unhelpful thoughts and behaviours in the first place; after all, it's likely that you'll have been doing those same things since childhood.

Learnt Helplessness

Learnt helplessness is the term used when someone

shuts themselves down from doing or being something else; instead, mistakenly believing that they can't do it, that it's out of their control or they are no good at it.

We can fall into learnt helplessness for several reasons:

1. We try to do something, and it doesn't work out, so to avoid further pain or disappointment, we decide never to try again; shutting down any possibility of making that 'thing' work in the future.

2. We get told something negative about our ability or personality either as a child or adult, subsequently believing it to be true.

3. We don't want to take responsibility because if we do, we'll have to take action. Often this occurs when we believe that something is outside our control and that we can't influence it, so there's no point even trying – incidentally, this is rarely the case. There's always *something* you can do to make a situation better.

4. We see someone else try to do something, and they fail for whatever reason. We then subconsciously decide that we can't do it either.

5. We perceive that something is too hard or that we can't do it, so we don't even try.

6. We adopt our parents/caregivers' learnt helplessness behaviours, e.g. if either parent shuts down when they feel overwhelmed, there's a good chance we'll do the same in similar situations.

Hearing things like, 'You're no good at maths/sport/English/reading' or 'You'll never amount to anything', can be particularly harmful to children and adults, especially if the person doing the 'telling' is in a position of perceived power, e.g. parent, teacher, boss.

I work with many clients who got told that they would 'never succeed' or were 'rubbish' at something as children and it's turned into a self-fulfilling prophecy. *We have to be consistent with our view of ourselves*, and therefore, we will look for and inevitably find ways to back up the thought implanted in our subconscious by a careless person.

Incidentally, if you weren't good at something as a child, there's a chance that you didn't get taught in a way that your brain accepted. We all learn in different ways; that's why you probably resonated with some teachers more than others; they taught in a manner that you identified with and understood.

The Spiral Effect

Our thoughts tend to spiral upwards when we're happy

and in a good mood and downwards when we aren't. *Like attracts like.* Therefore, when we have positive or negative thoughts, we tend to attract more of the same – creating a spiral effect.

Unless we do something positive to halt the flow of our less desirable thoughts, they can often spiral out of control, leading to low mood, feelings of overwhelm and at worst, stress, anxiety and depression.

However, you can always halt a downward spiral by consciously monitoring your thoughts and changing negatives ones as soon as you notice them. I'll explain how to do that later in the book.

Reticular Activator

The Reticular Activator System (R.A.S.) is a part of the brain that is like a 'seek and find' missile! Once you place your attention on something, for example, if I said, 'look for everything blue in the room' then asked you to close your eyes and describe everything green, unless you know the room well, it's likely that you will struggle. That's because you had unconsciously instructed your R.A.S. to just look for blue items.

We are bombarded with millions of pieces of information daily. If we didn't have a way of sorting through it and focusing on the essential things, we would quickly become overwhelmed. When we focus on something in particular, we subconsciously instruct our brains to sift through all incoming information and highlight/make us aware of things that match it.

Often when we consider something to be a coincidence, it rarely is, it's your R.A.S. in full flow. For example, if you buy a new dress or a suit, all of a sudden, you may see it everywhere when you've never actually noticed it before. That's not a coincidence; it's happening because you've activated your R.A.S. and it's drawing your attention to where you've instructed it to focus.

To illustrate how powerful your R.A.S. is, I recently had a client who wanted to change career direction; he planned to move from being a business development manager to a music producer. During one of his coaching sessions, we discussed how he might make the transition. One of the things we discussed was getting some formal training. On the way home, he heard an advert on the radio (the same radio channel he always listened to) selling a year-long programme at a local college teaching, yes, you guessed it, music production!

He said that he must have heard that advert dozens of times throughout its run, but it hadn't registered with him until now. His subconscious mind hadn't picked up on it until he had activated his R.A.S. by discussing his love of music production in detail with me.

In summary, your reticular activating system is the part of your brain that looks out for the things important to you. When you focus consciously on something in detail, chances are you'll see more of it – that's why visualisation is an excellent tool for activating your R.A.S., helping you find and get what you want which is particularly useful when problem-solving.

Internal Vs External Focus

Externally orientated people will look to others for advice, permission, and validation; they prefer getting told what to do rather than making their own decisions. They like to hear that their idea is a good one before they will take action. They typically:

- Look to others for answers.

- Seek advice from others

- Like to talk to others about their problems

- Tend to go with the consensus

- Take longer to make decisions.

- Worry what other's think

- Prefer to be 'told' what to do

- Like to get external validation

On the other hand, internally orientated people are much less likely to look to others for advice or guidance but will go inside themselves for answers. Characteristics include:

- Going on a gut feeling/using intuition

- Not needing other people's advice to make a decision.

- Not requiring permission from others to do something they want to do

- Making quicker decisions

- Rarely need external validation.

- Rarely worry about what others think.

These examples explain why some people will make decisions by themselves (internally) without asking for outside input; which can be frustrating for the externally orientated people. Similarly, it can frustrate the internally focused when someone takes too long to make a decision because they are waiting for the input from others, slowing down the process. Neither is right or wrong – they're just different! Create New Habits

It used to be thought that if we repeat any thought or action for 21 days, it becomes a habit; that's now increased to 66 days, and some research indicates the optimum repeat time is 100 days. As already discussed, the more we do something, the deeper the neural pathway becomes, making it automatic; with repetition, it becomes a habit.

Nothing worthwhile ever comes without *some* work. Therefore, if you become frustrated or sometimes forget to apply the techniques you learn from this book, don't beat yourself up or get disheartened. Simply either start again or continue where you left off and be aware that the more you repeat a thought or action, the easier it will become, and over time, you will create new habits. After all, when a baby learning to walk falls, you don't stop them trying again!

Tune In, Bliss Out...

As I've already said, the techniques here have been tried and tested thousands of people. They are simple and easy to use, and I've intentionally designed them that way because if you had to think about them, you probably wouldn't do them.

The hardest part of using the information I've included will be 'recognising' old unhelpful thoughts and behaviours, and remembering to apply these techniques. You've likely been running those old patterns for a long time and, as a result, you're brilliant at them!

Start by tuning in to your negative thoughts or feelings. Notice where you are and what's going on around you when they occur. Keep a notepad with you or jot them down in an App such as Microsoft's 'To-Do' or in the notes section on your phone. When you do this, you'll begin to notice triggers (whether it's people or situations), that set off that particular thought or action, we called this a 'habit loop'.

Once you're aware of your triggers, you can anticipate them and actively decide how to respond, using the different techniques in this book to avoid or stop any negativity before the downward spiral begins.

N.E.T. – No Extra Time

N.E.T. means maximising what time we have by doing two different things at once.

Examples of N.E.T.:

* Listening to Podcasts or audiobooks as you're doing other things such as exercise, emails, housework, on long car/train journeys/commuting.

* Making calls (safely) during long drives or train

journeys.

- Taking the train instead of driving so that you can work, read or do something creative.

- Reading a book while you're on a treadmill/static bike/Stairmaster, etc.

Conclusion

I have only briefly covered these topics; providing you with a high-level overview of their meaning. If you are interested in learning more, I suggest reading my first book, *'Thoughts Become Things: Change Your Thoughts, Change Your World',* available on Amazon in Kindle or paperback versions. Visit the book website for more information:

http://thoughtsbecomethings.co.uk

Jo Banks

1 - You Create Your Thoughts!

Most people don't consider where their thoughts come from and subsequently, live their lives at the mercy of their outdated thinking habits.

Your thoughts aren't plopped into your mind by some superhuman being - **YOU CREATE THEM** – every last one. They are based on your values, beliefs, rules and the programming/conditioning you received growing up.

They aren't fixed and commonly aren't even an accurate reflection of reality; they mirror your 'perception' of what you believe is real.

Depending on how deep a thinker you are, research has shown that we have around 60,000 thoughts every day, and up to 95% of them are the same as the ones we had the day before. So, if you're a negative thinker, it's no wonder you feel bad!

However, once you are aware that you create your thoughts, you can consciously choose to control them, rather than letting them control you. The hardest part is recognising that they are negative in the first place! Once you start gaining control of your thinking, your whole life can change for forever.

2 - Change Your Thoughts

You can't have two thoughts at once, it's impossible. Therefore, when you consciously tune into your thoughts, notice and change the ones that aren't serving you, you'll instantly feel more positive and in control. To change your thoughts:

1. Shout 'STOP!' and consciously switch your focus, to something more positive.

2. Create a go-to 'happy thought'; something that makes you smile, e.g. lying on a sun-drenched beach or a past event that evokes good feelings. As soon as you notice the negative thought, consciously replace it with the 'happy' one.

3. Wave the thought away. It may seem simple, but it works brilliantly. Couple that with singing the Frozen theme tune, 'Let It Go' can be particularly effective!

4. Get up and move - *motion creates emotion*. When you alter your physiology (body language), you instantly change how you feel.

These are called 'pattern interrupts'. Each time you interrupt your old patterns of thinking or behaviour, you reinforce the new one.

3 - Thoughts Become Things

'What we think about comes about.' Our lives are a reflection of our repetitive, automatic thoughts. Happy people have happy thoughts, leading to more positive and fulfilling lives. Negative people have the reverse. The ONLY difference between the two is in their thinking, and what we think is a CHOICE!

Contrary to what most negative thinkers believe, positive (or lucky) people experience precisely the same adverse conditions and situations as they do. The difference is, they don't allow themselves to become overwhelmed or defined by it.

As a result, positive people typically don't fall into learnt helplessness. They are more resourceful; ask better questions; look for solutions, seek out others who can help them. In essence, they take responsibility for their lives.

Whatever we consistently think about *is* our reality, whether it's true or not. If your life isn't going as well as you'd like, take note of your consistent and persistent thoughts. If they're predominantly negative, that's what you will be attracting into your life: THOUGHTS BECOME THINGS!

4 – The Stress Response

When we experience strong negative emotions in reaction to a real or perceived threat (such as worrying), we trigger The Stress Response. Our brain releases cortisol and adrenaline to give us a short burst of energy, enabling us to run, fight or freeze (see MM No 77). Over time, these neurochemicals not only build up in our bloodstream, but they can become addictive.

We can also become addicted to 'happy hormones', e.g. runners often crave the neurochemicals (endorphins and dopamine, etc.) that get released due to exercise.

When you feel stressed, anxious, or overwhelmed for any length of time, your body gets used to adrenaline and cortisol production. Subsequently, when you start to manage your emotions (using this book's techniques), these chemicals' release will reduce.

In response, your brain may attempt to 'create' stress (e.g. via a worrisome thought) in an attempt to force the release of the stress chemicals it is craving. When that happens, recognise it for what it is; acknowledge it, then let any negativity go. The techniques from MM No 2 – Change Your Thoughts will work for this.   (More on neurochemicals in Part 4).

Like Attracts Like.

5 - Like Attracts Like

Have you ever noticed that if you're in a bad mood, things tend to spiral and you end up attracting more negative thoughts, people and situations to you? It's not a coincidence; in fact, it's quite the reverse.

For example, you start the day feeling positive and upbeat, but one negative thing happens, like stubbing your toe on the dresser. Before you know it, your day deteriorates into a ball of negativity.

'Like attracts like' is a universal law; whatever energy you put out (positive or negative) you will attract more of the same back.

Therefore, it's essential to be conscious of your thoughts, changing any negative ones as soon as you notice them. Recognising thoughts that aren't serving you is the difficult part; changing them is relatively easy.

We can't always control what happens to us, but we can control how we respond. When you consciously CHOOSE to be optimistic and practise positive expectation, i.e., things will work out well; you will undoubtedly begin to attract more positive things to you.

6 - Real Vs Imagined Thoughts

Our brains can't tell the difference between something real and something vividly imagined; this is incredibly important to know. When you vividly imagine something, positive or negative, your brain interprets it as factual, and you experience all the associated emotions and feelings with that thought, good or bad.

To explain, when you read a book, you aren't physically experiencing what you're reading, and yet you *feel* like you are; you may laugh, cry, get angry, but it isn't physically happening to *you*.

Suppose you're a negative thinker or someone who excessively worries, imagining worse case scenarios in minute detail. Your mind interprets those worries and fears as being real. When that happens, it triggers The Stress Response (our primal fight, flight, freeze response) releasing biochemicals into the bloodstream, which can, in the long term, have adverse effects on your health.

Make a conscious decision to halt your negative thoughts and focus on what you want rather than what you don't. As you do this, you will be conditioning your nervous system for success rather than failure. The more positive you think, the more positive you'll feel.

7 - Automatic Thoughts

Automatic negative thoughts are habitual and persistent, making them seem more believable; they result from unconsciously creating deep neural pathways in the brain. The more you have a particular thought (positive or negative), the deeper the neural connection becomes making it easier to access. After a while, it becomes automatic.

To combat negative automatic thoughts, practise tuning into your inner dialogue. As soon as you recognise any negativity, stop and challenge your thinking. Ask yourself:

1. Is this thought true?
2. How do I know it's true? What evidence do I have?
3. What is a more realistic thought?

When you stop and challenge your negative thoughts, create a pattern interrupt. Each time you interrupt that old habit, it's like scratching a CD, it won't play the same again, and you'll be able to create new, more realistic thoughts. Over time, the new connection will deepen creating a new automatic thought – hopefully, a more positive one!

8 - Distorted Thinking Patterns

Unhelpful thinking patterns (or cognitive distortions) are ways that your mind convinces you that your thoughts are real, without any actual evidence. These distortions reinforce negative thinking, giving us false confirmation that our thoughts are rational and accurate. Distorted thinking includes:

1. Black/white thinking – discounting shades of grey.
2. Over-generalising – seeing a negative situation as evidence that everything is negative.
3. Jumping to conclusions – making a negative interpretation or prediction without proof.
4. Magnifying or minimising – thinking something is better or worse than it is.
5. Discounting positives – purely focusing on negatives.
6. Mindreading – believing you know what others are thinking about you.
7. Labelling (self and others) – assigning an emotive label, even where there is evidence to the contrary.

Again, being aware of your internal dialogue is crucial. Check any negative thoughts against this list and actively challenge any distorted thinking, replacing it with something more realistic. Look out for any patterns.

9 - Changing Distorted Thinking

Distorted, unrealistic thinking patterns can often result in worry, upset and overall general negativity. In the extreme, it can lead to depression and anxiety disorders.

We don't wake up one morning with distorted thinking. It's typically conditioned/programmed; built up over many years. However, it's rarely a reflection of reality.

Distorted thinking can also become automatic. As with 'automatic thoughts' described in MM No 7, we can use a similar set of questions to break them down, allowing us to analyse whether they are accurate. If you recognise that you may be distorting your thinking, ask yourself the following questions:

1. Which distortion am I applying (see MM No 8)?
2. What evidence do I have that it's true?
3. What is a more realistic thought?

Once you bring consciousness to your thoughts, recognising where you may be distorting them, you can interrupt those patterns by actively *choosing* more realistic ones to replace them.

The mind can't tell the difference between something real and something vividly imagined.

10 – Repetitive Message Thoughts

If you keep having the same negative thought or you're worried about something repeatedly, check to see if it carries a message. Is there something you need to do, or some lesson you need to learn or heed, but you're just not doing it?

A thought with a message or where an action is required will keep coming back until you do something about it. Trying to avoid it or hoping that it will go away, rarely works; it keeps coming back for a reason.

Therefore, where possible, you should deal with it immediately, or if it's not something you can resolve that day, put a plan in place and then choose to stop worrying about it, safe in the knowledge that you have it under control.

If a repetitive thought doesn't have a message, it's likely to be an automatic one, i.e. you've had it so often that you don't even have to think consciously to create it. If that's the case, you can change it using any of the techniques mentioned in MM No 2, Change Your Thoughts. Remember, you create your thoughts, and, therefore, you can control them, changing any that aren't serving you for more realistic ones.

11 – Get Curious

Our thinking styles and reactions to people and situations are typically learnt when we are children, up to the age of seven. After that age, our brain functioning changes. We learn our thoughts and responses in two different ways; firstly from our primary caregivers and secondly through trial and error.

As adults, unless we make a conscious decision to do something different, we will think and behave in the same way we did when we were children.

One of the things that I like to do when I recognise that my thoughts and reactions are a little 'off' is to get curious about them. I'll ask myself:

1. Why did I think that?
2. What was the positive intention behind that thought?
3. What triggered it?
4. Was my reaction valid?
5. Was there a better way to deal or think about it?

Our brains will continue to think and react automatically until we bring some conscious attention to it. Often, that focus allows us to recognise when what we're doing isn't serving us, making it much easier to change.

12 – Managing Triggers

Recognising your triggers (or even that you have them) is a great tool to gain control over negative or distorted thinking. Often, certain people or situations trigger an adverse reaction in us, which we may not necessarily be aware of.

For the next three days:

- Tune into your internal dialogue, and notice anything negative that you say to yourself, especially when you get a negative feeling about a person or situation.
- Write it down and note what was going on around you that could have triggered it. Was it something someone said, something you read or just an errant thought that popped into your head or is it a thought you repeatedly have, i.e. an automatic one? Include as much detail as possible.

Within three days (you can do longer if you wish), you'll likely start to recognise patterns in your thinking and behaviour.

Once you're aware of what those triggers are, you'll more able to pre-empt them and create effective plans to deal with or avoid those people or situations altogether.

13 – Excessive Worry

Excessive worry can be incredibly debilitating, and yet, it's so unnecessary. As I've said previously, *the mind can't tell the difference between something real and something vividly imagined* and so, what you're worrying about feels real, even though it may not be. Some studies suggest that up to 95% of what we fear most never happens – that's a whole lot of worry for nothing!

To combat excessive worry, try these three solutions:

1. Write your worries down and create a plan for what you might do to overcome them *should* they arise. Everything always feels bigger when it's in your head. Getting worries down on paper often provides much-needed clarity and rationality. Be on the lookout for any distorted thinking patterns, MM No 8.
2. Allow yourself no more than 15 minutes a day to worry; sit somewhere uncomfortable, and set a timer.
3. Save all your 'worries' for one day a week, e.g. 'Worry Wednesday'. Sit somewhere uncomfortable and set a timer, again allow no more than 15 minutes to worry.

If you choose Nos 2 or 3, avoid making a note of your 'worry items'. That way, it's likely that you'll forget all about them when your allotted 'worry time' arrives.

14 - Reframe Negatives

Reframing is a powerful tool. It basically involves refocusing your attention; actively looking for positives rather than dwelling on negatives.

There are always at least two ways of looking at every situation; however, if you're more pessimistic than optimistic or you're a constant worrier, chances are you'll automatically look for negatives.

To reframe, ask yourself empowering questions, e.g.:

- What could be good about this?
- What else could this mean?
- What's a more positive way of looking at this?
- How can I use this to my advantage?
- Who can help me with this?

When you ask yourself powerful questions, it often helps move you to a more resourceful state, allowing you to *see things as they are, not worse than they are.* Reframing also helps undo the old, outdated programming (learnt behaviours) that no longer serve you. Consider keeping these questions visible and using them each time you encounter a seemingly negative or difficult situation.

What we think about comes about.

15 - Change Your Perception

A situation is just that, a situation; it's entirely neutral. It's the meaning we put to it that makes it positive or negative, and we get meaning from our filters.

We develop our filters (values/beliefs/rules) initially through our early programming (watching and copying our primary caregivers), latterly, by our life experiences.

When you take a step back from a negative situation and challenge your initial perception, you'll likely find that you were reacting automatically to a specific stimulus, i.e., producing a 'programmed' response.

However, you can override outdated conditioning by actively *choosing* to reframe and asking empowering questions such as, 'What could be good about this?'

You often can't stop a situation from happening, but you do have full control over what it means to you, how you feel about it, and how you react. It's a matter of challenging your old perceptions and conditioned reactions and consciously choosing to think and act differently. Each time you do, you'll either be creating a new neural pathway or deepening an existing one.

16 - Choose Your Mood

Have you ever got up in the morning in a good mood, only for something relatively small to happen, triggering a negative downward spiral? It's unlikely that the situation itself caused you to feel bad, but rather what you subconsciously thought about it.

Each morning, when you wake up, actively *choose your mood*. Consciously decide how you want to think and feel and regularly check in with yourself throughout the day to ensure that you're sticking to it. If something negative happens (which it inevitably will) you can *choose* not to let it affect you. Note it down as a trigger, and then let it go.

Also, be aware that you affect the people around you with your mood (positively or negatively) as *behaviour breeds behaviour*. Whatever emotion you are experiencing, you will be emitting through your physiology and others will pick up on it; we don't even have to say anything for people to guess how we're feeling. No-one wants to be thought of as a 'mood hoover', a 'doom monger' or a 'psychic vampire' nor do we want to spend time with someone like that, so be mindful how you might be impacting on others.

17 - Choose Happiness. Now!

Happiness is a choice. Your happiness does not depend on anything or anyone external; it is inside you right now! Many people mistakenly believe that they will finally be happy when they achieve or attain something outside of themselves, e.g. the ideal partner, baby, divorce, marriage, new house/car/kitchen/bathroom, different job or promotion, etc.

When we project our happiness into the future (i.e. when we say or think, 'I'll be happy when...'), we create strong neural pathways, conditioning our nervous system to believe that happiness will always be in the future. But that isn't true. You can be happy now if you consciously choose it.

Practising gratitude is a great way to tap into your innate happiness. According to new clinical studies, creating a habit of acknowledging the positive things you have in your life and feeling genuinely thankful for them, alters our brainwaves. Start a gratitude journal, each morning/ evening note down three things for which you're grateful. Take a moment to visualise them, feeling the gratitude you have for each one, as you do this; you will condition yourself for happiness NOW.

18 — Ignore Others' Opinions

I love the saying, *'what others think of me is none of my business'*. Many of us limit our lives (potential and opportunities) by worrying about what others' *may* think; this is one of the most common distorted thinking patterns (MM No 8). It is often referred to as 'mindreading', i.e. believing that we know what others think about us without any evidence.

While we spend valuable time and energy worrying about others' thoughts and opinions, we potentially miss great opportunities. It's also important to note that *we are the centre of our own universe*, and while we're busy worrying about others, it's likely that they haven't even given us a second thought. Most people are busy getting on with their own lives and being the centre of *their* universe!

Whenever you attempt something new or different, *someone* will judge you for it; that's just how people are. However, if the judgement is harsh, it says far more about them than it does about you. They may be suffering from insecurity, jealousy, or low self-esteem, which your drive and positivity have brought out in them. Do a reframe, and use that knowledge to move you into action.

19 — Pleasure vs Pain

Our brains were designed to move us away from pain and towards pleasure. It is a D.N.A. based, fundamental survival need, reaching back to our ancestral caveman times.

Our brain's ultimate function is survival at all costs; to keep us alive long enough to procreate. That's it; nothing else is as important as that. We are neurologically wired to that end.

Therefore, in every situation, our subconscious weighs up the perceived level of pain that 'thing' might produce, explaining why we often procrastinate. Delaying action is our brain's way of attempting to prevent pain.

For example, it's likely that people who choose to Netflix binge over exercising, on some level associate exercise with pain. Others may perceive being overweight and unhealthy as more painful than vegging out in front of the TV, so they choose to exercise.

If you find yourself procrastinating ask, 'What's the perceived pain I'm trying to avoid here?'. It's a simple way to start recognising your values (what's important to you) and moving out of learnt helplessness and into action.

20 - The Past Does Not Equal the Future

Many people limit themselves by mistakenly believing that they can't do, be or have something based on past experiences; this can be consciously, or subconsciously driven.

Subconsciously, you may find that you self-sabotage without realising why. Alternatively, you may procrastinate, finding the flimsiest reasons not to do something. Both are avoidance methods; your brain's way of steering you away from pain. You may also *consciously* decide not to do something thinking, 'I've tried that before, and it didn't work, so I'm not trying again'. It's another way of evading perceived pain.

However, just because something didn't work out in the past, does not mean that will happen again. Situations change; people change, YOU'VE changed. I'm guessing that you aren't the same person you were five years ago.

You can break old patterns of thinking and behaviour by getting curious (see MM No 11). If you are self-sabotaging or procrastinating, sit quietly and ask yourself what you're scared of; what perceived pain you're trying to avoid? Getting clear allows you to get past learnt helplessness and move you into action.

Motion creates emotion.

21 - You Get What You Believe

Whether you think you can, or whether you think you can't, you're right! If you believe that you can't do something, likely, you will shut yourself off from even trying – it's the unconscious mind's way of protecting you from potential pain. However, much of what you believe has nothing to do with reality but is a result of your conditioning.

For example, as a child, you may have had risk-averse parents; subsequently, you're reluctant to try new things as a grownup. Or a teacher may have told you that you were rubbish at a particular activity or subject and you still believe that to be true today. Alternately, as an adult, you may have tried something, it didn't work out, so you convinced yourself you couldn't do it or it wasn't possible for you.

We have to remain consistent with our view of ourselves; as a result, we and look for examples to back up what we believe to be true and act in ways that reinforce them.

Start challenging your old, potentially outdated beliefs about what is or isn't possible for you and remember, *the past does not equal the future*. Get curious, reframing negatives and take action. Every journey starts with the first step.

Jo Banks

22 – Beating Procrastination

Self-sabotage and procrastination can be described as misguided self-love; our mind's way of protecting us from things it perceives as harmful or not in our best interest. They come from the pleasure/pain theory, described in MM No 19.

'The Five-Second Rule' is a great way to bypass the part of the brain that creates the excuses that stop us from taking action, that could lead to potential pain.

There is a five-second lag between having an idea and acting on it. During that short time, your subconscious will calculate if there's any perceived pain or risk (if you don't want to do something, it's 100% likely to find some!). It will then come up with multiple plausible excuses not to do the 'thing', and the moment will be lost.

To circumvent it, as soon as you have the idea to do something, count down out loud '5-4-3-2-1' and immediately launch into physical action. It is a simple but incredibly powerful tool. Once you move, you'll find that momentum will carry you forward as *motion creates motion.* (Credit to Mel Robbins, The Five-Second Rule).

23 – Procrastination Types

There are two types of procrastination, 'productive' and 'destructive'. On the whole, productive procrastination can be positive, as our brains need time to wander; to figure things out and have space to develop creative ideas and solutions.

'Destructive' procrastination, on the other hand, is closely linked to stress. The subconscious needs to feel good immediately as relief from feelings of stress, anxiety and overwhelm. In this case, it's much harder to get into action as it isn't just the task you *should* be doing that's stressing you, it's likely to be something deeper, e.g. anxiety about your job, children, money, etc.

We commonly use numbing activities such as online shopping, gaming, Netflix binging, drinking, etc., in an attempt not to have to think about what we *should* be doing. 'Numbing' can be advantageous for productive, short-term procrastination but can be a sign of larger issues if it's excessive or long-term.

Take a critical look at how much time you spend doing 'numbing' activities; it can indicate deeper problems that require closer attention. Doing a time audit can be helpful with this – MM No 65.

24 — Set Boundaries

People will treat you how you allow them to. If any of your colleagues, friends or loved ones continually mistreat you, it's likely because you're letting them. If you don't challenge or set boundaries, others will assume their behaviour is OK.

I realise that for some of us, dealing with potential conflict can be incredibly difficult or even feel unsafe, especially if you identify with being a people-pleaser. However, the longer you allow bad behaviour to continue, the more acceptable you make it and the worse it will get.

If you think someone is mistreating you, you must talk to them. It doesn't have to be an aggressive exchange (which tends to happen when we let things build up). Get clear about what you want to say and the outcome you want and practise saying it aloud before having the actual conversation. Visualise everything going perfectly, and you'll be conditioning your nervous system for success.

It's important to remember that *the people who argue and complain when you set boundaries are typically the ones that have the most to lose.*

25 - The Power of Visualisation

I can't stress enough the power visualisation has on our lives, as *the mind can't tell the difference between something vividly imagined and something real.* The more time you devote to imagining the outcome you want, the more likely you will achieve it. It's a proven technique widely accepted in sports psychology, yet it's rarely discussed or used in everyday life.

The great thing about visualisation is that it's easy to do, you can do it anywhere, and no-one needs to know you're doing it! Vividly imagining scenarios creates new neural pathways in the brain in the same way as it would if you were physically doing the thing you're picturing.

Get into the habit of imagining positive outcomes, especially in potentially stressful, upsetting or difficult situations. Picture them in as much detail as possible; see what you would see, hear what you would hear and feel what you would feel if everything were to go perfectly.

This simple exercise significantly increases your chances of success. When the actual situation that you've been imagining occurs, your subconscious will go into autopilot, allowing you to act instinctively in a way that will deliver the outcome that you've vividly pictured.

Jo Banks

Part 2 — Take Control

Jo Banks

26 - Manage Your Inner Critic

Have you ever actually listened to your internal dialogue? It's the background commentary to your life, and yet, unless someone points it out, you may not even realise you have it. However, we have more conversations with ourselves than we do with anyone else - ever!

Stop for a minute and listen to what your internal voice is saying. Is it kind and loving, or nasty and cruel? Is it positive or negative? Better still, ask yourself the question, *'Would I let someone else speak to me the way I'm speaking to myself?'*

It's important to remember that YOU create your internal self-talk. If it is pessimistic or destructive, it's *you* saying those things; it isn't reality. It's merely a byproduct of outdated programming and automatic thoughts.

If the voice is negative, alter its intensity by changing the pitch, tone or accent; change it to something you find funny, e.g. Donald Duck, Mickey Mouse or a complaining, whiny teenager. When you do this, you automatically adjust the feelings/emotions associated with it. Alternatively, simply say, 'STOP' and immediately change your focus to something more positive. Remember, *we can't have two thoughts at once*.

27 — Embrace Change

Change is THE one constant in our lives, yet most of us struggle and fear it more than anything else. However, change doesn't have to be negative; without it, we wouldn't push ourselves to grow and move forward.

If you're struggling with a significant change in your life, e.g. job loss, break up, illness, try analysing what's going on and seek ways you can reframe it.

Ask yourself some powerful questions to help move you out of learnt helplessness and into a more resourceful state. For example:

- How can I use this to my advantage?
- What can I see that could be positive about this?
- How do I need to think and feel to transition through this quickly?
- What actions can I take to resolve this positively?
- Who's been through or going through this who may be able to help me?

Take decisive action and get moving; two of the quickest ways to gain control and transition to a resourceful state. Remember, *everything happens for a reason*; although it's not always immediately apparent at the time.

28 - Control What's in Your Control

There are only three things that you can control:

1. Your thoughts (what you're saying to yourself)
2. The images you create in your mind.
3. Your behaviour

Trying to control anyone or anything else is a waste of valuable time and energy and typically leads to pain. You can't control the other individuals, the weather, the traffic, your health, but you can control how you think and respond to people and situations.

Focus on what's in your sphere of influence. Identify any challenges, and ask yourself some great reframing questions, e.g. what could be good about this? Who can help me with this?

Wherever possible, create a structured, workable plan to resolve problems. You may need to try different approaches, but that's OK. Not everything works the first time. Don't be discouraged; keep trying until you find something that works.

Having a plan and taking consistent action will give you a better sense of control and help you move forward with positivity.

29 - Get Clear

If you have a challenging situation that requires a solution, or a goal that you want to achieve, but you don't know where to begin, start by getting clear about all aspects of it. When we're unclear, things seem bigger and more daunting than they actually are; resulting in procrastination, self-sabotage, worry and anxiety. If something appears to be too big, it's less likely that you'll follow through.

Get your thoughts out of your head and onto paper; things often seem far worse than they are when they circulate in our heads. I realise that technology has now overtaken handwriting. However, I still prefer an old-fashioned pen and paper as our brains remember 700% more of what we physically write down.

When you get your thoughts out of your head, problems often seem less complicated and overwhelming, making it easier for you to analyse and organise them into a workable, step by step plan. Take action towards your goal (no matter how small) that same day, and you'll automatically activate your Reticular Activating System; the part of the brain that helps draw your attention to specific things that are important to achieving your goal.

66

Change your thoughts, change your world.

30 - Choose How You Want to Feel

There are five things that that you can do to alter how you think and feel instantly:

1. Change your physiology (body language). What we do with our body reflects our thoughts. If you want to feel better quickly, change your body language to the emotion you want to feel.

2. Change your focus. Reframe negative situations by actively seeking potential positives.

3. Change your beliefs – *Whether you think you can or whether you think you can't, you're right!* Challenge your old beliefs and seek new, empowering ones.

4. Change your language – We *'feel'* the language that we use. If you want to be less stressed, angry, resentful, overwhelmed, etc. stop using words that make you feel that way. Swap them for something lighter and more positive.

5. Ask better questions – Use empowering questions to reframe. Questions such as what could be good about this? How can I use this?

Whenever you're feeling less resourceful, choose one of these tools and make a conscious effort to work on it consistently for the rest of the day.

31 — Victim vs Owner

Are you a victim or an owner, lucky or unlucky? We typically fall into one category or the other, usually as a direct result of our upbringing, e.g. if you had pessimistic parents, the likelihood is that unless you've made a conscious decision to change, you'll consider yourself unlucky as an adult. As *we have to remain consistent with our view of ourselves,* we continually look for evidence to back up our view of ourselves, and we'll inevitably find it.

Countless studies have produced overwhelming evidence that people who consider themselves lucky are happier, healthier, and wealthier than their 'unlucky' counterparts. However, the same amount of adversity happens to them as it does to their negative counterparts. The difference is that the 'lucky' ones CHOOSE (consciously or unconsciously) to see things differently. Their unwavering optimism makes them more resourceful and resilient; allowing them to think more clearly and make better choices.

To swap from pessimism to optimism, start by being grateful for what you have, get into the habit of reframing negative situations, and STOP TELLING PEOPLE THAT YOU'RE UNLUCKY – view it as an outdated story!

32 – Pity Parties

'Pity Party' is what I refer to when I see people practising extreme self-pity (I can instantly identify with it because that used to be me!).

When I think back to all the great things that I had in my life, yet I still insisted on indulging in such unhealthy behaviour, it makes me cringe. I was a real victim, *choosing* to see only negatives, not even realising that it was a choice.

Once you understand that your life hasn't been 'done to you'; the results you're experiencing right now are due to your past thoughts and actions (or lack thereof), you can start to take steps to turn things around. It's never too late.

Tune into your behaviour. As soon as you notice that you're complaining or going into 'pity party mode', STOP; recognise it as an outdated programme and change it; even if you're mid-sentence.

Use the pattern interrupts from MM No 2. Think about something that makes you happy (you might want to pre-prepare a list, as often it's hard to think of things when you're on a negative spiral). Alternatively, get up and move, change your physiology; *motion creates emotion.*

33 - Take Responsibility

As we've already seen, we can't control what happens to us, but we can control how we react. The quality of your life right now is a direct result of your past thoughts and actions.

As much as you may want to blame someone or something else, e.g. partner, parents, spouse, children, economy, politicians, etc., for your current circumstances; YOU are ultimately responsible.

You have made decisions and choices which have brought you to where you are today. Taking ownership and responsibility for your life, empowers you to take decisive action towards achieving what you want, rather than blaming others and aimlessly drifting, accepting the life you *think* you've been given.

If things aren't as you would like them to be, DO SOMETHING ABOUT IT. Stop waiting for someone or something else outside of you to change or to do it for you. Decide what you want, create a plan and take immediate action. Remember, every decision you make today (even the small, seemingly inconsequential ones) are shaping your future. Your life is in your hands.

34 – Better Decision Making

Using your intuition is a vital part of the decision making process. Of course, you should critically analysis options; however, if you balance the final decision between both facts and intuition, you're far more likely to get a better result.

Our gut feeling is a fantastic barometer for whether we're on the right track; it is another D.N.A. based survival tool, specifically designed to keep us safe. Our subconscious can take in far more information than our conscious mind. It can process millions of pieces of information within seconds, whereas our conscious can only manage five.

When you make the right decision, you'll feel lighter. If you don't, then the chances are that the decision isn't the right one. When we're in tune with our higher calling or values, there is a lightness to our correct choices; a calmness, an internal 'knowing' that we've made the right decision.

If that lightness isn't there, it may be worth revisiting your decision. Give yourself some time out; stop thinking about it, go for a walk, sleep on it, do something different. Giving your brain space, allows you to become 'unstuck, allowing room for you to *feel* what's right.

66

We don't learn by talking, we learn by listening.

35 - 'People-Pleasing'

Children who grow up in households were love, validation and attention are lacking, often subconsciously adopt people-pleasing behaviours in an attempt to fill the emotional void.

While such behaviour can serve a purpose as a child, it can become debilitating in adulthood. People-pleasers often put others' needs and wants, far above their own, which can ultimately lead to exhaustion, anxiety, depression, and low self-esteem.

If you think you may fall into the people-pleasing category, the following questions can help you to start to understand your motivations and break old, unhelpful habits:

1. Am I doing this because I want them to like me?
2. Am I doing this because I'm expecting some sort of reward - like someone telling me how great I am?
3. Am I doing this to please someone else? If so, am I OK with that?
4. What do *I* get from doing this?

Taking a critical look at the reasons behind why you do certain things can be a real eye-opener – get curious.

36 - Learn to Say 'No'

Being able to say 'no' is an issue for many people, none more so than for people-pleasers. We'll often hear ourselves agreeing to something even though we don't want to do it, seemingly unable to stop.

A negative result of being unable to say 'no' can mean an increased workload, going places you don't want to go, doing things you don't want to do and even being taken advantage of by others. Like anything else, saying 'no' can take some practise:

1. Start by saying 'no' to at least one small thing every day for a week. Practise makes perfect and getting used to saying 'no' to small things, builds your tolerance and confidence.
2. Stop worrying about what other people think. Most people won't think twice if you say 'no' as long as you do it in the right way.
3. Avoid apologising; you don't have to say sorry for taking responsibility for your own life.

Saying 'no' when it isn't normal for you can be a little daunting at first; it may even provoke some negativity in others. However, the more you do it, the easier it will become.

37 - Comparing Yourself to Others

If you're familiar with the 'Iceberg Model', you'll know that what you see from a person's actions and outward appearance is only a tiny part of what's going on underneath.

While another person's life might look idyllic, we rarely know what's *really* going on. By trying to be like them, we unwittingly cause ourselves unnecessary stress, trying to live up to something that isn't even accurate.

Unfortunately, social media has given us unrealistic expectations of what we should all be, do or have. We get constantly bombarded with everyone else's seemingly 'perfect' lives. In truth, people only post what they want you to see. As a coach, when I meet a client for the first time, I'm often shocked at how different the reality is to how they portray themselves on social media.

You are unique; there is no-one else in the whole world like you, who has your particular set of skills, experience, and outlook – why would you want to be like someone else? Be your own person and focus on your journey and what *you* want to do, be or have, and your life will become far more fulfilling.

38 – Stop Asking For Permission

Many of us don't reach our full potential because we continually seek permission, approval or validation from others before thinking we can take action.

The problem with needing those things is that people always have their own agenda. They will give you advice based on *their* perception, filters, needs and wants, which may differ from your own. They may even have a conscious or subconscious need for you to fail.

I've met many people who haven't achieved their goals purely because someone has else put them off. They got told that they weren't good enough, their idea wouldn't work, or some other negative reason why they shouldn't or can't do it. As a result, they didn't even try, shutting themselves off from the possibility of achieving what they set out to do.

You don't need the approval of others. By all means, ask their opinion, but tune into your intuition. YOU know if something is right for you; you don't need someone else to tell you. Trust yourself. You know better than anyone else what you're capable of, give yourself a chance. You may be pleasantly surprised by what you can achieve.

39 - Perfectionism

Another reason why many of us fail to reach our full potential is due to perfectionism. If you're a perfectionist, trying something new without knowing the exact outcome, can be anxiety-inducing.

I know plenty of people who either don't start or never finish their book, project, training, qualifications, etc. not because they aren't capable but because they can't live up to their own exacting standards, and sadly, give up.

I heard a saying recently that I thought summed this topic up perfectly: *instead of striving for perfection, strive for excellence.* I love this because no one can be perfect, but *everyone* can be excellent! It's a great reframe.

I tend to lean towards perfectionism, especially when it comes to writing. I wouldn't publish anything because I was so scared of making mistakes and being judged harshly. That was until I realised that I was still achieving far more than any of the people who criticised my minor errors; their judgement then became irrelevant.

If you recognise yourself as a perfectionist, reframe and work towards being excellent. It will help move you out of learnt helplessness and into action.

We have the answers to all our problems
within us.

40 – Limiting Beliefs

Our limiting beliefs are stories that we've developed over time to justify why we can't do something. We learn our limiting beliefs in three ways:

1. Through our early programming, e.g. we may have heard, 'People like us don't do things like that.'
2. Through trial and error, e.g. trying something which didn't work out, so we convince ourselves that it's not possible.
3. Through something we got told by someone else, e.g., 'You're no good at X.Y.Z.'.

These limiting beliefs are often based on fear; it's our subconscious' way of keeping us out of pain. In some cases, they can be completely irrational, e.g. being scared of all dogs, because one barked near you as a child or frightened of spiders because your mum was scared of them. The more you tell the 'story' about the limiting belief, the more real it becomes in your mind, and you begin to act in a way that backs it up.

Start to challenge your limiting beliefs by getting curious about their origin. Exposing yourself to the 'thing' you're scared of is an excellent way of confronting your fears and overriding your automatic, programmed response.

41 - Change Your Story

Storytelling generates powerful emotions within us. We often use 'stories' to justify our limiting beliefs and explain why we can't achieve our goals. Stories like:

- I've tried before, and it didn't work.
- I don't have the qualifications.
- I can't do that because of my children/partner/job.
- I'm too busy.
- I don't have enough money.
- I'm unlucky/things never work out for me.
- People like us don't do things like that.

Essentially, they are excuses, dressed up as bona fide reasons. After all, there are plenty of other people with similar, if not worse challenges who have overcome tremendous adversity to achieve extraordinary things.

- What stories have you been telling yourself about why you haven't achieved your goals?
- Who would you be and what would you have without your story?

Maybe NOW is the time to re-evaluate, and replace those old, outdated stories with something more compelling and empowering!

42 - Stop Complaining

Complaining is an insidious habit which is not good for us or those around us. Start to take notice of the thoughts you're having and how you communicate them. If you recognise that you like to complain, start to make a conscious effort to stop by tuning in to what you're thinking and saying and change it.

Your subconscious mind listens to everything you say, and if you are consistently negative (especially when there's no real need to be), that's how you will feel – *where focus goes energy flows*.

When you notice that you're complaining, ask yourself some empowering questions:

- What's really going on here? Is it as bad as I think? Is what I'm saying/thinking true?
- What can I see that could be positive?
- What do I need to do to turn this into a positive?

When you CHOOSE to stop complaining, you'll also be far more pleasant to be around. Humans naturally gravitate away from negative people and towards positive ones (away from pain and towards pleasure). Be someone that people want to be around, not avoid!

43 – The 'Negative Competition!'

It's essential to be alert when you find yourself in the company of negative people, as it's incredibly easy to get influenced by their distorted thinking, and unwittingly pulled into their drama.

One specific thing to be mindful of is getting drawn into a *'my life is worse than yours'* competition. We've all done it at some point; someone starts telling you how bad their life is and you respond with, 'You think that's bad, listen to this…!'

We learn this kind of behaviour in the playground – you remember the arguments we had as children, where the kid that could end with, 'Well my dad's a policeman!' was the winner? Well, the *'my life is worse than yours'* competition is the adult version.

If you find yourself competing in this way, stop and think, 'Is this something I want to win?' I know I don't! I'm more than happy to let someone else beat me at that game; no matter how competitive I am.

Step aside and graciously hand over the metaphorical winner's trophy to the other person, and walk away with your self-esteem and positivity intact.

44 - Watch Your Language

The words we use consistently, are extremely powerful and affect the overall quality of our lives. When you use negative, unempowering language not only does it make you feel bad, but it can also limit your success.

Unfortunately, many of us have got into the habit of using overly dramatic or negative language, even when the situation doesn't call for it. As a result, we can turn a relatively mild experience into something much worse, just through the use of inappropriately strong or harsh language.

Our language also massively impacts our outcomes. I can instantly tell whether an athlete will win a race based purely on what they say. For example, if they use words like 'try' I know they've no chance of winning. 'Try' is a weak word which indicates that you don't believe that you can do it. Swapping 'try' for 'I'm going to' is far more convincing to your subconscious.

Over the next few days, tune into what you're saying to yourself and others. Consciously replace strong, emotive or negative language with something less potent and more empowering. By doing that, not only will you feel better, but you'll be more likely to achieve success.

"

Whether you think you can or whether you think you can't, you're right!

45 - Avoid Using 'Don't'

Our brains do not recognise the word 'don't' when we use it as a command. As a result, our subconscious delivers the exact opposite of what we intended. For example, when you tell someone, 'Don't do X, Y, Z', do you marvel at the fact that they do the exact thing that you've just asked them not to do? I'm sure you've also done it yourself; how many times have you touched paint when you've seen a notice stating, 'Don't touch. Wet paint'?!

The same thing happens with our self-talk. If you tell yourself, 'don't fail', 'don't get upset, 'don't drop that' typically, you will do the very thing you're trying to avoid.

To stop this, flip your sentences, consciously stating commands (for both for yourself and others), in positive terms, removing the word 'don't' from the request. For example, instead of saying, 'Don't trip!' say, 'Walk carefully.' Rather than, 'Don't drop that!' change it to, 'Carry that with both hands.' Swap, 'Don't fail', for, 'I can do this'.

You are far more likely to get what you want (from both yourselves and others) if you state requests in the positive. It's a simple but incredibly effective tool which doesn't take much effort but gives great results.

46 - Change How You Feel About Someone

We can't always get along with everyone, that's just life. However, we often get 'stuck' with people we wouldn't ordinarily choose to be around; this can sometimes lead to conflict and unnecessary upset.

I often hear, *'You can't change others, but you can change yourself'.* I think that's only partially true. Technically, you can't change others; however, because your thoughts affect your behaviours, you automatically respond differently to someone once you change how you feel about them; as a result, they *have* to change in response. It's an automatic process which occurs in the subconscious.

The quickest and easiest way to do this is to visualise the person looking and sounding differently. Alter their appearance and the sound of their voice, e.g. give them Micky Mouse ears, Ronald MacDonald Hair, a distinctive walk and a Donald Duck quack (the funnier, the better).

Practise visualising that 'modified' person repeatedly in as much detail as possible and notice how your feelings change toward them. When you feel differently, you'll behave differently. They may not be able to pinpoint what's altered, but likely they will change as a result.

47 – Breaking the 'Rules'

It's likely, that the people you spend the most time, with both at home and work, have similar values to you, as we get naturally drawn to individuals (and companies) whose morals and standards match ours.

However, conflict can occur where we have the same values but different rules around how we 'live' them. For example, think of all the rules your family has around Christmas and the conflict that can occur when two families come together following marriage.

Our 'rules' typically come from generations of conditioning. However, it doesn't mean that ours are right, and others' are wrong; they're just different. The next time you find yourself locking horns with someone, but you know you have the same values, e.g. loyalty, trust, integrity, take a closer look at your rules – likely you'll find that they are different.

The good thing about rules is that you can change them. You don't have to continue living with outdated ones that no longer serve you; simply make new ones. Remember, compromise is vital in any relationship, and as long as your values are similar, the rules you apply to them may not be as important as you think.

48 - Accept Others Default Styles

Many people have different values and rules than we do. Although it can be frustrating, it doesn't mean that they are wrong, and we are right; we're just different.

For example, you may have a friend who is consistently late, which drives you crazy. You may have tried everything you can think of to get them to turn up on time – to no avail. You may even have the same value of 'respect'; however, your rules around how you 'do' respect are different. If you keep getting upset and angry with them when you know that's their default behaviour; then it's *you* that has the problem, not them!

You can, however, *decide* how you want to react when it happens. You know what they will do beforehand, so it's up to you to manage your emotions or put plans in place to ensure that it doesn't spoil things for you.

No-one can make you feel a certain way; nobody has that amount of power. It's your programming that you use to interpret others' behaviours that influence your emotions and reactions. Don't be held captive to your old, outdated conditioning. You can actively choose how you want to react – STOP GIVING AWAY YOUR POWER TO OTHERS (see MM No 95).

49 – Managing Constant Criticism

There's a huge difference between constructive feedback and constant criticism. Unfortunately, certain toxic personality types get a kick out of making other people feel bad for no reason. If you're on the receiving end, you may find that you start second-guessing yourself, avoiding things you want to do. In the long run, it can affect your confidence and self-esteem.

The irony typically, the person doing the criticising, does it because of their own feelings of low self-worth; by putting you down, they make themselves feel better. When you know this about someone, you can anticipate their reactions, which puts you in a position of power. When you can have an educated guess about how they're likely to react, you can plan for it.

To counteract others' unhelpful criticism:

1. Have a bet with yourself about exactly what they are going to say and when. Forewarned is forearmed!
2. Don't rise to it. Instead, smile because you saw it coming all along!
3. Think of some positive responses. You don't have to be nasty, but you can be firm if you plan ahead.

50 - Imposter Syndrome

Imposter syndrome is something pretty much everyone experiences at some point. Some manage to get over it relatively quickly, for others, unless they address it, it can stay with them their entire lives.

In my experience, there are two primary triggers:

1. Finding what you do easy, which makes you think that you must be doing it wrong, and at some point, you'll get found out. Usually, this is because you grew up believing that work should be hard. However, if you find something you love, and that comes naturally to you, it won't necessarily be hard.

2. You find yourself in a job or at a level of seniority that at some point, you could only aspire to. Although you know you can do it on a subconscious level, your insecurities come to the surface and you literally 'wait to be found out'.

Imposter syndrome is typically a result of our early programming, the stories we tell ourselves, and our limiting self-beliefs. Getting curious about where your thoughts and feelings originate, is a great way to understand your outdated drivers; once you're aware, it's easier to change to something more realistic.

Jo Banks

Part 3 — Achieve More

Jo Banks

51 - Design Your Life

If you don't consciously create your life, you can't be surprised if it doesn't turn out as you'd hoped. Everything you have right now results from your past thoughts, decisions and actions; your life hasn't just 'happened' to you. So, rather than leaving your future up to chance, instead, design it:

1. Decide what you want to do, be or have in your career, health, finances, relationships, etc. Write them down, stating them in the positive, i.e. what you want rather than what you don't want.

2. Brainstorm all the things you could do, the actions you could take, to achieve your goals – avoid editing at this point.

3. Analyse each potential solution critically, and choose the ones that seem most viable. 'Chunking' similar activities together is a great way to get started without feeling overwhelmed.

4. Set achievable timescales and take action on at least one thing from each category immediately, by doing that, you'll trigger your R.A.S. to be on the lookout for items related to your goal.

5. Regularly check your progress and revise your plan or actions if necessary.

52 - Set Authentic Goals

Your goals should be authentic, i.e. not things you think you *should* have or someone *else* wants you to, but because they are important to you.

Authentic goals are not just about achieving 'something'; they are about how you grow and the emotions you during all stages of the process, e.g. sense of achievement/fulfilment, etc. When goal setting:

1. Make your goals SMART – Specific, Measurable, Attainable, Realistic, Time-bound. Achievable time scales are critical; *a goal without an end date is a dream!*

2. Be clear on *WHY* you want them. If the WHY isn't big enough, it's unlikely that you'll follow through. You may need to dig deep on this one, but it's critical. Typically we want something because of the emotion/feeling we've associated with it. Establishing your WHY will also help you identify if the goal is authentic.

3. Sharing your goals with someone else increases the chances of achievement. Consider finding an accountability partner – someone else who also has tangible aims. Check-in with each other regularly to update on progress and bounce ideas around.

53 – Create a Plan

Creating a plan for each of your goals is critical if you're serious about achieving them. It should have clear steps/actions that you're going to take together with workable timescales. A goal without a plan is unlikely to happen, as 'life' will take over.

1. Create a top-level, yearly plan containing everything you want to accomplish in that year (*you don't need to wait until January to do this – you can start anytime*). It doesn't have to be detailed; headings are adequate.

2. Distribute your goals evenly over the four quarters; that way, you won't feel overwhelmed. Also, our internal reward system works better with shorter-term goals.

3. Take your goals for the first quarter and break them down into 3 x monthly targets.

4. Break your monthly goals down into a more detailed 4-weekly plan. You may also wish to do the same each week for daily activities.

There are some great products available that will help you plan effectively. I've already mentioned that I use the 'Self Journal' from Best Self; it helps keep me focused. But remember, planning tools only work if you do!

54 - Take Consistent Action

One of the main differences between those who succeed and those who don't is ACTION. Successful people typically try more things over a more extended period, than their 'unlucky' counterparts.

Those who succeed *choose* not to give up when they experience failure. Instead, they keep going, trying different alternatives, knowing that the more consistent and persistent action they take, the better the results will be. After all, Edison made 10,000 lightbulb prototypes until he discovered one that worked. J K Rowling, the author of the famous 'Harry Potter' franchise, was initially rejected by twelve publishing houses; yet, thankfully, both kept going until they achieved what they set out to do.

If you take consistent action but fail to achieve your goal, it doesn't mean that you're a failure or that what you did wasn't good enough; it simply means that the action you took wasn't right.

Try something else, and if that doesn't work, try something else and keep trying until you find a solution. Many people give up just on the brink of a breakthrough, avoid that being you.

A goal without an end date is a dream.

55 - Why Goals Fail

How many times have you made a New Year's resolution or set a goal and not achieved it? It's believed that up to 92% of New Year goals get abandoned by January, 15th; they typically fail because:

1. The goal isn't 'authentic' (see MM No 52).

2. The 'WHY' isn't big enough. Remember, our brains' primary function is to keep us away from pain and move us toward pleasure. Therefore, if the discomfort of doing what's required is worse than the perceived benefits, you're unlikely to follow through.

3. You believe that you don't have enough resources, e.g. time/money/expertise, etc.

4. You have limiting self-beliefs or an old 'story' about why you can't be, do, have that 'thing'.

5. It's outdated, so you no longer want it; usually, because you've taken too long over its achievement. Regularly review your goals and ditch the ones that no longer make you feel excited. Typically we can cling to outdated dreams because we perceive letting go as a failure. However, ultimate failure is holding on to something you no longer want, and constantly berating yourself for it.

56 – Feel the Fear – Do it Anyway!

If you have the idea to do, be or have something, it's likely that you already have everything you need within you to be able to achieve it. If you didn't, you probably wouldn't have the thought in the first place, and yet so many people fail to even get out of the starting blocks.

Typically, I hear excuses like, 'I'm waiting for the right time' or 'I'm waiting for a sign'. Well, here's the thing, there's rarely a right time, and if you're looking for a sign, THIS IS IT!

Most people fail to achieve or even begin to pursue their dreams, not because of timing, but due to FEAR. Fear of:

- Failure
- Being judged
- Being unable to complete it
- Looking foolish
- Change
- Hard work

Everyone has fears; those who choose to feel the fear and do it anyway tend to be more successful. When would NOW be a good time to start working on your goals?

57 - Model Success

The quickest way to achieve your goals is to model someone who has already done it. You can save an incredible amount of time, money, and energy by emulating others. It enables you to quickly discover what works and what doesn't without going through the pain of finding out for yourself.

If you know someone personally, contact them, arrange coffee (you must pay!) and pick their brains. Most people will be more than happy to help (unless, perhaps, you're going to be in direct competition with them) as it's flattering when someone is interested in you and what you've achieved.

If you don't know anyone, but you know it's been done before, research it. We have no excuse now as everything we need, on virtually any topic, is at our fingertips with books, YouTube and Google.

Incidentally, don't be put off if you want to start a new venture, and find someone else is already doing it; simply reframe:

1. It means that there's a market for it.
2. No-one will be able to do it quite like you!

58- Create A Morning Routine

For many of us, mornings can be chaotic. However, how you start your day, sets the tone for the rest of it. Creating a positive morning routine or ritual (that you stick to, even at weekends), is an excellent way to program your mind for success. Following is a list of some of the activities you could incorporate:

1. Positively visualise your goals and how you'll feel when you achieve them.
2. Set your intention/outcome for the day.
3. Visualise the day ahead going perfectly.
4. List three things for which you're grateful.
5. Choose the mood you want to be in for the rest of the day (positive vs negative; it's a choice).
6. Read a few pages of a book that inspires you.
7. Practise yoga/ meditation.
8. Go for a 15-minute walk.
9. Enjoy a wholesome breakfast.

By creating a positive morning routine, you consciously decide how you want your day to be, rather than being at the mercy of other people's moods and demands. You may need to set your alarm 15-minutes early, but it will be worth it.

59 — Check Your Phone After Breakfast

For many of us, the first thing we do when we wake up is to reach for our phones; checking our emails, the news and what's been happening on social media while we slept.

By doing this, we let the outside world in before we've even had a chance to wake up fully; we inadvertently open ourselves up to others' views, demands, stresses, etc. before our brain has had time to ready itself.

Humans were not designed to have that amount of information bombard us as soon as we open our eyes, and our brains can find it difficult to cope. As a result, we can inadvertently trigger the stress response (fight, flight, freeze) even before we've managed to crawl out of bed, which significantly reduces our resilience.

If you delay checking your phone, at least until you're out of the shower (better still, wait until you've had breakfast), you'll give your brain the time it needs to acclimatise to being fully awake. That way, you'll reduce stress, and increase your resilience, enabling you to choose your mood, and set your intention for the day, rather than being at the mercy of others' demands right from the start.

Strive for excellence rather than perfection.

60 - Plan Your Day

At the end of each day, take ten minutes to plan what you want to achieve (and all the related activities) for the following day. You will accomplish far more by doing this, as you'll be less likely to procrastinate, wasting time deciding where to start and being at the mercy of outside influences.

Be crystal clear about the outcomes you want, i.e. what you must complete, to make the day a success. To keep yourself on track, you may want to list actions hour by hour. You could even go one step further and set reminders on your phone; which is a great way to stay focused.

Of course, there will be interruptions, but often we attend to them at the expense of what we *should* be doing. If you find yourself getting sidetracked without good reason, ask yourself, *'Does this task take me nearer or further away from my goal'.* If the answer is 'further away', stop what you're doing and refocus.

Each time you complete a task, cross it off your list; and you'll trigger your internal reward system. At the end of each day, check your progress and create your plan for the next day, carrying over any outstanding activities.

61 - The Power of Lists

Lists are a great way of staying focused and achieving more. As I've said before, *what gets written down gets done*. When we get things out of our heads, they often don't less daunting.

Writing things down physically, i.e. using a pen and paper is preferable, as we remember 700% of what we physically write due to the new neural pathways we create. However, some great virtual tools and apps are available for 'list' purposes to help you get more organised.

The Microsoft To-Do app is a great way to keep track of day to day tasks. It's especially beneficial if you work in teams as you can share actions with others; allowing everyone to update and tick off activities as they complete them.

I also fully utilise the 'Reminders' app on my Apple products and use a daily planner, which I spend five minutes completing each morning and evening. These tools allow me to plan effectively and provide a constant reminder of my short and medium-term goals. Without them, I can tend to drift, working on what I *want* to do rather than what I *need* to do.

62 – Do Your 'Ugly' Tasks First

When planning your day, schedule the worst/difficult/ important tasks first. We humans, tend to put off anything that we perceive to be difficult, complicated or too time-consuming as we associate it with pain, resulting in procrastination.

When we delay these tasks, we often spend the rest of the day fretting about the fact that we haven't done them, often carrying them over until the next day and thinking about them all through the evening. *We can spend more time worrying about not doing something than it would take to do it!*

By scheduling and completing your difficult jobs first, not only will the rest of the day feel like a breeze, but you'll also release dopamine (the Reward Chemical) which will give you a real sense of achievement. It's important to note that most tasks are not as bad once we start, and take far less time than we initially thought.

Single-mindedly working through a task until you complete it, is a significant contributor to success. If you struggle with procrastination, try using the Five-Second Rule, that I discussed in MM No 22 – Beating Procrastination.

63 — Chunk Your To-Do List

I realise that if you're exceptionally busy, as most of us are, when you create a long list of everything you need to do, it can seem overwhelming. That's where 'chunking' comes in'.

When you've written your list, chunk 'like' activities together, e.g. group all your calls under one heading, your emails under another and personal tasks together, etc. whatever makes sense to you.

Once you've done that, start firstly with the 'chunk' containing your ugliest, most important task first and get straight into action. Avoid letting your procrastinator's brain kick in; use the 5-4-3-2-1 'Five-Second Rule' and jump into action. J.F.D.I. (Just Flippin' Do It!), and avoid giving your brain time to find excuses.

Use N.E.T. (No Extra Time) to combine tasks and make things more enjoyable, e.g. exercise with a friend, listen to inspirational podcasts as you work, etc.

When you find ways to make your routine or difficult tasks enjoyable, you will begin to retrain your brain for happiness, triggering those all-important 'happy' hormones; endorphins, dopamine, serotonin, etc.

64 - Identify Your Avoidance Habits

We all have avoidance or 'numbing' activities that we use for procrastination purposes. These activities can be beneficial in small doses, giving your brain a much-needed break from other tasks. However, in excess, they can sign deeper problems, such as stress, anxiety, depression. Numbing can include:

- Watching TV – Netflix binging is hugely addictive. We sit hours on end until we've watched all the episodes of the latest 'must-see' series.
- Internet surfing – Whether it's watching YouTube, online shopping, reading the news, etc. when we surf the net, it's like a different time zone; minutes can turn into hours in the blink of an eye.
- Gaming – Desperately trying the complete the next level before we allow ourselves to do what we should be doing or going to bed.
- Undertaking relatively unimportant tasks – Cleaning cupboards, clearing desks, or endlessly checking social media accounts.

What avoidance or numbing habits do you use? When you're conscious of them, they are much easier to change for something more constructive and productive.

If you have an idea to do something, you have what it takes to achieve it within you.

65 - Complete a Time Audit

One of the biggest reasons clients cite for not completing their goals is lack of time. However, many of us have much more of it than we think. Conducting an audit is a great way to understand how you spend your time and where you could maximise it.

To do this, use a day to a page diary, e.g. Google's 'day planner' is ideal for this, print some copies off and keep a note of *everything* you do (not just work-related tasks) and how long they take. Aim to do it for a minimum of three days, including a Saturday or Sunday.

Once you've completed the exercise, search for the areas where your time could be better utilised. You'll be amazed how much time you're wasting without realising it. Pinpoint the areas for improvement (e.g. where you may be 'numbing' or doing tasks that you could outsource), and schedule activities that would be more beneficial, e.g. Me Time (MM No 96).

Finding just one extra hour a day will add up to 7 hours a week, 30 hours per month, which equates to 15 x 24 hour days per year; imagine what you could achieve in that amount of time!

66 - Outsource!

If you find that time is tight, and you're struggling to get everything done, costs permitting, look for ways to outsource activities, i.e., paying someone else to do them for you.

Some clients struggle with outsourcing. Typically, they grew up in traditional households, were paying someone to do simple but time-consuming tasks would be against their conditioning. However, we are now in very different times, and life is far more complicated; time is at a premium.

If finances are not a blocker, but you're still hesitant to outsource, ask yourself what your time is worth to you. Calculate your hourly rate versus how much it would cost to pay someone else; you may find it's a no-brainer. Tasks that are ideal for outsourcing include:

- Ironing/ cleaning/ gardening/ car valeting/ decorating/ household odd jobs.
- General household admin, e.g. booking holidays, making travel arrangements, paying bills, making appointments, etc. You can find a virtual PA very easily online, and they can be very cost-effective (remember to take up references).

67 – Get Time Smart

If outsourcing isn't a viable option for you, get smarter with daily activities:

- Automate your bill-paying - set up standing orders and Direct Debits wherever possible so that you don't have to remember to pay bills.
- Do your banking online (if you don't already).
- Fully utilise online shopping for groceries as well as clothing, shoes, general goods.
- Look for areas where you can use N.E.T. (No Extra Time) where you can do two things at once, e.g. if you frequently drive, use your journeys to make calls (safely) or listen to an audiobook, podcast or self-help programme.
- Batch cook food and freeze it rather than cooking from scratch each meal or eating ready-made supermarket food.
- Have clothes ready for the week ahead so that you don't have to think about what to wear each day.

Involve your family in household tasks – delegate – it teaches kids valuable life skills. Getting them to take responsibility isn't mean or cruel; reframe, see it as preparing them for the future.

68 – Working From Home

Since COVID, more of us are working home than ever before. While it does have its benefits, it also has its downsides; not least, the lack of differentiation between home and work. Being accessible 24/7 can quickly become overwhelming unless you set boundaries for both yourself and others. Here are some tips for gaining back some control and making it work for you:

1. Be strict about your start/ finish time – our productivity declines significantly after 8-hour's work. Avoid the temptation to turn your laptop on outside those times.

2. Take regular breaks - get up and move away from your desk – change your physiology!

3. Take a 15-minute walk at lunchtime – it will clear your head, release happy hormones making you more productive.

4. Set agendas with expected OUTCOMES for virtual meetings – you'll find the time is better utilised.

5. Drink plenty of water – we tend to forget to drink when we're at home.

6. Turn off notifications - the temptation to look at the latest alerts interrupts flow and productivity.

69 — Chunk Problems Up

Regularly I see clients overwhelmed because they are projecting worse-case scenarios well into the future, worrying about things that may never happen. None of us can know how things will turn out for sure; the best we can do is deal with what we know right now.

When an issue arises, especially if it's complicated with many variables, instead instantly jumping to conclusions or panicking, chunk it up. Look at what you can realistically do, right now. Take it step by step, and one action will naturally lead on to another.

You don't have to have the answers to the overall problem right from the start. Simply have an idea of how you would like the outcome to be and deal with what's in front of you right now, adjusting your actions as things unfold.

After all, a SatNav doesn't give you all the directions at once; you get them individually. It adjusts the route as obstacles, such as traffic jams, arise. Treat your problems in the same way. Deal with one aspect at a time, altering your approach in response to the results you experience, doing more of what works, and less of what doesn't.

When you set boundaries, the ones with the most to lose will be the most upset.

70 - Choose Your Outcome

We waste so much time doing things without considering *why* we're doing them. For example, how many meetings have you attended and at the end thought, 'What was the point of that?' When you get clear on your outcomes, you'll find that you will achieve far more. For example:

- If you need to have an awkward or difficult conversation, decide the result you want first and design questions to help you achieve it.
- When you send an email, consider the outcome. Do you want the other person to take action, or are you merely passing on information? To avoid disappointment, and extra work, be clear on what you're asking for; set expectations and outcomes.
- When arranging a meeting, establish what you want to achieve by the end. If you're unclear, the other participants will be too.
- When you visit or call a friend, what's your intention? Are you just going to hang, to help them, to make them feel 'special' or all three?

By consciously choosing your intention or outcomes, your actions will produce more powerful results, and you will be making more of your most valuable asset, time.

71 - Ask for Help

If you find things are getting on top of you, (at home or work), please seek help as soon as possible. Avoid putting it off in the hope that things will get better; they rarely do. Many people mistakenly believe that asking for help is either a sign of weakness or that others are too busy for us. However, we ALL need a little help from time to time; even the most successful achievers.

Speak to someone who you know will keep your confidence – often a good chat with a friend over coffee can sometimes be all you need. However, if your problems are more complex, find a coach or a therapist who can help you make sense of what's going on and help you create a workable plan.

As a coach, I know the power of getting things out of our heads. Often just something as simple as saying what you're thinking out loud (especially to someone who has no vested interest in the outcome), can help you to gain much-needed perspective. Things can feel much bigger when they're in your head. If you're feeling particularly stressed or overwhelmed, please speak to your doctor or healthcare professional. There is no stigma attached; they will not judge you, and there's lots of help available.

72 - 'Shoulding' All Over Yourself

When you say that you *should* do something, the chances are that you have no real intention of doing it! Should is procrastination language; it literally shuts us down from achieving what we set out to do.

For example, when you say, 'I *should* be writing that report', 'I *should* be doing the laundry', 'I *should* be exercising', you have no real intention of doing it!

There is a saying in N.L.P. (Neurolinguistic Programming) circles, 'Stop *shoulding* all over yourself.' We spend so much time procrastinating, talking about all the things we *should* be doing, that we fail to deliver a fraction of what we're capable of achieving.

Instead, choose to consciously remove the word from your vocabulary and replace it with positive intention. For example, 'I am going to....', 'I will...' and you'll be much more likely to achieve your goals.

Incidentally, when we use *'should'* about others, e.g., 'They *should* do this' or 'You *should* do that', we are typically judging; forcing our rules on them and potentially imposing unrealistic expectations.

73 – Small Questions

Many of us fail to notice the number of small questions we ask ourselves daily. Questions like, 'What will I have for breakfast/lunch dinner today?', 'Shall I eat that chocolate?', 'Should I go for a walk?', 'Should I have that important conversation with my boss/partner/child or should I Netflix binge instead?' (Notice the word 'should' in there?!)

When you start taking care of the small questions, you can potentially avoid larger problems in the future. Consider this; nobody, wakes up one day overweight, in a lousy relationship, hating their jobs, and in debt, etc.

Those things are typically the result of making bad choices over many months or even years, failing to recognise the importance of seemingly unimportant small daily questions and answers.

Start tuning in the questions you ask yourself and the decisions you make throughout the day. When you bring consciousness to your thoughts and decisions rather than being on autopilot, the chances are that you'll begin to make better choices. Make the small questions count.

74 — Do Something Different

Einstein said that the definition of insanity is, *'Doing the same thing over and over again and expecting a different result'*. Yet, so many people expect things to change with minimal or no effort on their behalf. That might be the case in some instances; however, on the whole, things don't get better until we do.

If you continue to do the same things repeatedly, you can't realistically expect a different outcome. I must use the saying *'Always do what you've always done, always get what you've always got'* a dozen times a week to clients expressing concern at their lack of progress. However, it's usually abundantly clear that they haven't put any effort whatsoever into changing anything.

If you want something to be different (a situation, a person or yourself), *you have to do something different*; the responsibility lies with *you*. That may mean altering your thoughts, feelings, behaviours or taking alternative actions to those you've taken previously.

This book is packed full of tools and techniques to help you do just that. However, if you aren't prepared deviate from your 'normal' pattern and routine, you can't expect things to change.

75 - Trust Your Intuition

Start to tune into your gut feeling (intuition). It is your internal guidance system, designed to keep you safe. Humans developed this primal safety mechanism early in our evolution to protect us from potential harm, and it's still very much in operation today. However, we often override or dismiss it altogether, choosing instead to rely on what we *think* rather than what we *feel*.

Your intuition can be far more accurate than anything you could learn externally or rationalise through your conscious thought processes. *If something feels wrong, it probably is.* Your subconscious deals with thousands of pieces of information in seconds, whereas the conscious mind can only process five. However, the only way it can communicate that something's wrong is through feelings, e.g. something may feel slightly 'off', but you may not be able to describe what that is.

Start tuning in to how you feel about a person or a situation. It's still important to consider facts, but do that *in conjunction* with your gut feeling and your decisions will be far more sound. Your intuition is there for a reason; ignore it at your peril!

Jo Banks

Part 4 – Increase Your Well-Being

Jo Banks

76 – The Stress Response

As we learnt in Part 1, *our minds can't tell the difference between something real and something we vividly imagine.* When we experience negative emotions such as stress or anxiety, whether real (hearing footsteps behind us on a dark night), or imagined (worrying about our job security), our brains react in precisely the same way; firing off the stress response (i.e. fight, flight, freeze) – MM No 4.

Biochemicals, adrenaline (norepinephrine) and cortisol get released into the bloodstream giving us a quick burst of strength and energy to enable us to deal with the threat.

It is a DNA based response dating back to our caveman times when we had to either fight sabre tooth tigers, run away or freeze until the danger had passed. Although it is still a valid reaction to physical threat today, it isn't helpful for 'perceived' threats, e.g. worrisome thoughts that trigger stress and anxiety.

We can lower the effects of the stress response by managing and controlling our thoughts; however, the quickest way to reduce the biochemical impact is to use them for what they were designed for, physical exercise!

77 – Stress Neurochemicals

When we experience stress, adrenaline (norepinephrine – the flight/fight/freeze hormone) gets released immediately. It increases our heart rate and focusses our attention; giving us a 15-minute burst of energy, to enable us to deal with the immediate 'threat'. Physical symptoms include tightness or fluttering in the chest, butterflies, light-headedness and inability to concentrate on more than one thing.

Secondly, cortisol (the Stress Hormone) gets released. It regulates the bodily functions that aren't crucial at that moment, e.g. immunity, digestion and growth, reproductive functions.

Over time, if unused, these two chemicals build up in the bloodstream, suppressing the immune system. Ultimately, their accumulation can result in physical illnesses, e.g. diabetes, heart problems, etc., and mental health issues, e.g. stress, anxiety, depression, etc.

Therefore, it's critical to manage your stress levels. You can do that by learning to control your thoughts and taking adequate exercise, which actively burns off the excess neurochemicals.

78 – The 15-Minute Walk

One of the quickest and most effective ways of reducing the stress response is through exercise.

Just 15 minutes walking each day (preferably outdoors) is clinically proven to reduce the effects of stress, anxiety, and depression. When you increase your heart rate for a minimum of 15 minutes, you will use up the stress hormones (adrenaline and cortisol). After all, they are there to give us a quick burst of energy!

Not only will you effectively utilise those neurochemicals, but you will release 'happy' hormones, including endorphins, serotonin, and dopamine. If you exercise with someone else or in a group, you also release oxytocin (the 'love' hormone).

Everyone can find 15 minutes in their day; take a break at lunchtime or after work. Schedule it in as you would any other important meeting. Not only will you feel better, but you will increase your brain functioning; giving you the ability to deal with problems and multi-task more effectively. As you walk, make sure that you look towards the horizon, which is clinically proven to reduce the adverse effects of stress even further.

79 – Stress Forces Narrow Focus

When we experience stress, our focus narrows; think of it like viewing your phone in portrait mode. Again, this is one of the side-effects of the stress response. Our brain is attempting to focus all our attention on the one significant 'threat' so that we can deal with it quickly and effectively.

The problem is that there is rarely just one thing causing us stress today; therefore, narrowing our view, is not helpful, often causing even more of it. Andrew Huberman, Neuroscientist at Stanford University, says that the quickest way to widen our perspective and reduce stress is walking or cycling OUTSIDE (sorry, if you're a treadmill or static bike junkie, it doesn't have the same effect!).

When we physically move forward outdoors, our view automatically widens; this is another throwback to our caveman times when we had to be aware of physical threats coming from all sides when we were out in the open. It's another excellent reason to schedule your 15-minute daily walk, focussing on the horizon (or as far ahead of you as you can see), widening your view from portrait to landscape.

80 – Hack Your 'Happy Hormones'

When we undertake certain activities, we release specific combinations of neurochemicals into the bloodstream. All of these chemicals have a purpose.

As well as the ones we emit when we are stressed, we release hormones in response to positive experiences.

Once you're aware of your 'happy' hormones, what each one is responsible for and how to trigger them, you can purposely choose to do the activities that force their release. Thereby enhancing your well-being and effectively combating stress and anxiety.

Building these activities into your daily routine will help you feel good from the inside out. Happiness does not necessarily come from anything external; it's something we can easily create within us by hacking our neurochemicals.

The four principal 'happy' hormones are dopamine (The Reward Chemical), oxytocin (The Love Hormone), serotonin (The Mood Stabiliser) and endorphins (The Pain Killer).

81 – Dopamine (The Reward Chemical)

Dopamine is the chemical that makes us feel good when we achieve something. You can hack this hormone by:

• Completing a task

• Ticking things off a list

• Doing self-care activities

• Eating good food (including chocolate!)

• Celebrating wins (even the small ones)

• Completing a challenging exercise workout

In childhood, we get strongly conditioned for reward following task completion, triggering dopamine from an early age. Likely your parents will have said things like, 'Finish your homework, and you can play', 'Finish your dinner, and you can have dessert', 'Tidy your bedroom, and you can have a treat', etc.

If you set your day up in the same way, i.e. reward yourself after completing a challenging task (that is not me giving you a free pass to eat chocolate by the way!), not only will you achieve more, but you'll feel good about it too! It's another reason why doing your ugliest tasks first (MM No 62) works so well; when you do, you release dopamine.

82 – Oxytocin (The Love Hormone)

Oxytocin gets released in response to physical touch or from being near others (humans and animals). It increases social bonding and helps us to feel physiologically 'safe'.

You can hack this hormone by:

- Hugging (if you can hug someone for 15-seconds or more, the effects get heightened – even more so if you're both naked!)
- Prolonged physical touching
- Exercising with other people
- Holding hands
- Playing with a baby
- Playing with pet
- Laughing with others
- Sharing experiences with others which generate strong emotions
- Massage
- Giving a compliment face to face

Oxytocin acts as a chemical messenger in the brain and plays an integral part in human behaviours, including sexual arousal, recognition, trust, anxiety and mother-infant bonding.

83 – Serotonin (The Mood Stabiliser)

Serotonin is responsible for several different internal processes, including sleep, regulating appetite, promoting learning and memory, increasing positive feelings and emotions.

You can hack your serotonin through:

- Exercise
- Meditation
- Massage
- Sun exposure
- Walking outdoors, especially in nature
- Eating wholesome, unprocessed natural foods, e.g. whole-wheat, oatmeal, brown rice and pasta, oily fish, fruit and nuts.
- Visualisation – vividly remembering happy times or creating a positive mental view of how you want your life to be

Serotonin deficiency is thought to be associated with several psychological symptoms, such as anxiety, depressed mood, aggression, insomnia, low self-esteem, etc. Therefore, it's essential to build activities into your daily routine that boost this vital hormone.

84 – Endorphins (The Pain Killer)

Endorphins minimise discomfort and pain and maximise pleasure. Recent studies suggest that they play an essential role in reducing stress, anxiety and depression and are critical to our overall well-being.

Since humans naturally seek to feel pleasure and avoid pain, we're more likely to do an activity if it makes us feel good. From an evolutionary standpoint, this helps ensure our survival.

Hack your natural endorphins by:

- Exercising (especially with others)
- Laughing (especially with others)
- Watching comedies
- Eating wholesome foods
- Eating dark chocolate and drinking red wine (in moderation!)
- Dancing and singing (even if you're not good at it)
- Helping others

We also release endorphins in response to unhealthy 'numbing' activities, e.g. Netflix binging, excessive gaming/online shopping, etc. It's essential to be mindful of where you're getting your endorphin hit.

85 - Create An 'Attitude of Gratitude'

Practising gratitude was once considered 'woo-woo' New Age nonsense. However, according to recent research from the science laboratories at Harvard and Stanford (amongst others), gratitude is proven to reduce depression, anxiety and stress, and increase overall well-being and happiness. The S.A.S. considers it so crucial to their operatives' mental health and well-being that they incorporate into basic training.

We can feel and express gratitude in multiple ways by thinking about:

- The past - retrieving positive memories and being thankful for elements of your childhood or past experiences.
- The present - not taking your good fortune for granted; focusing on what you do have rather than what you don't (abundance rather than lack)
- The future - maintaining a hopeful and optimistic attitude; positively visualising how you want your life to be in as much detail as possible.

When we focus on Gratitude, we release the dopamine, oxytocin, serotonin AND endorphins; it's simple to do and costs nothing.

86 – Practising Gratitude

There are different ways you can practise gratitude, including journaling, creating lists or simply visualising what you're grateful for in your mind. Creating a gratitude habit is a great way to start and end your day and doesn't take up much time or effort:

- Each morning, before you get out of bed (and before reach for your phone!), think of three things for which you're grateful. Create vivid pictures in your mind, make them big, bright, colourful and noisy and tune into the positive feelings they generate.

- Each evening, before you go to sleep, review your day and again, choose three things for which you're grateful. Evening gratitude also forces you to seek the positives in even the worst of days, often resulting in better sleep and overall positive mental health and well-being.

I recommend seeking new things each time you practice 'gratitude'; this will prevent you from becoming complacent. Research also suggests that the positive effects get heightened when we feel grateful for people and other non-materialist things, like helping someone with a problem.

87– Biological Rhythms

Our biological rhythms play out over 24-hours, corresponding to the Earth's rotation around the Sun. Our Ultradian Rhythm controls our sleep/wake cycle, heartbeat and digestion.

1. Our wake cycle:

    • Each cycle lasts for 90 minutes.

    • At varying times within each cycle, our concentration increases and decreases.

    • When you find yourself 'zoning out' or unable to concentrate, that is when your cycle is at its lowest.

    • Problems can arise when we ignore these ebbs and flows and try to maintain constant focus, attention and activity, failing to heed our natural need for a break.

2. Our sleep cycle:

    • Each lasts for 90 minutes, where we alternate between light, deep, and R.E.M. sleep (Rapid Eye Movement, which is when we dream).

    • We have approximately five cycles during a typical 7-8 hour sleep.

    • If you wake up in the night, it can take a full cycle, i.e. 90 minutes, to fall back to sleep.

88 – Wake Cycle

Using your Ultradium Rhythm to manage your day will reduce stress, anxiety and negative emotions and increase your productivity.

To use your biorhythms to your advantage:

- Start to tune into your natural 90-minute cycle, noticing when you are more/less productive or have a greater or lesser attention span. There will be a pattern to it.
- If you struggle to focus when you start work, it could be that you're in a lower phase of your rhythm. It won't last for long, but it may be beneficial to do something less demanding during the first 10-minutes or so.
- Try not to force concentration if you're struggling; instead, take a short 5-minute break; move away from your work station (if possible) and do something unrelated.
- Avoid napping during the day as it activates the sleep version of the rest-activity cycle.
- Taking a 15-minute walk at lunchtime or the end of your working day can help focus and attention. Go when you notice a dip in your levels of concentration.

89 – Better Quality sleep

When we are stressed or anxious, it almost always gets reflected in our sleep. We often wake up in the middle of the night, (typically after the second sleep cycle around 3.00 am), worrying about something that our subconscious has not been able to process satisfactorily. It can then take another full sleep cycle before we fall back asleep. If you suffer from disturbed sleep, try these tips:

• Keep a notepad and pen by the side of the bed. As soon as you wake up, make a note any worrisome thoughts. Typically that will be enough for your subconscious mind to consider the matter dealt with, and you will quickly drift back off to sleep.

• If you struggle to fall asleep, go to bed and wake up at the same time (even at weekends) for two weeks to reset your sleeping pattern.

• Set up a good bedtime routine; this could include a warm bath, drinking a warm, nonalcoholic/non-caffeinated drink, practising relaxation techniques.

• Ensure that the room is not too hot or cold and is quiet and dark. Avoid using electronic equipment half an hour before bed, as the blue light they emit has been proven to cause sleep disruption.

90 - Breathworks

The 'Physiological Sigh' is a clinically proven method that automatically calms the nervous system in times of stress. It triggers activation of the phrenic nerve to the diaphragm and causes your lungs to bring in oxygen.

We automatically do this when we cry and try to talk simultaneously; we also do it during sleep. You will also see your dog do it when it settles down to nap.

The 'sigh' re-inflates the little sacs in the lungs called the 'alveoli' which balances the carbon dioxide and oxygen in the bloodstream and lungs.

It's effortless to do, and you can do it anywhere:

- Take two inhales through the nose (until your lungs fully expand) and then release the air through one LONG breath out.
- Repeat two/three times, and you should see a significant reduction in your stress levels.

This technique is courtesy of Andrew Huberman (@hubermanlab) neuroscientist at Stanford University, USA.

Be the change you want to see in the world.

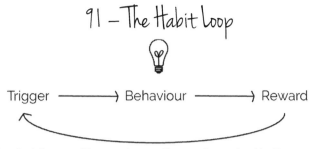

91 – The Habit Loop

Trigger ⟶ Behaviour ⟶ Reward

Our habits, positive and negative, get created in the same way and follow precisely the same process (above). Whenever we do something, it's because there is a perceived benefit; we may not be entirely conscious of what that is, but it doesn't mean it's not there.

Think of a habit that isn't serving you, e.g. worrying, overeating, procrastination, etc. and ask yourself:

1. What's triggering this?
2. What is the behaviour I do (mentally or physically)?
3. What reward do I get for this behaviour? (You may have to dig deep on this one).

This technique helps you identify when there isn't a valid reward, or where it may be outdated, allowing you to replace it with a BBO (Bigger Better Offer). The BBO could be something as simple as being curious (see MM No 11), or being kinder to yourself. When you get curious about your behaviours, it's much easier to change the ones that are no longer serving you.

92 - Practise Mindfulness

'Mindfulness' seems to be quite a buzz word at the moment. Dr Jud Brewer, a neuroscientist at Yale and MIT, has proven through his research that being mindful calms and relaxes the brain and decreases feelings of stress and anxiety.

Mindfulness is about being 'present' in the moment rather than worrying about the past or future. A great way to be more mindful is to take five minutes twice daily to tune in to what's happening around you. It could be when you're doing the dishes, cooking, driving, cleaning your teeth; when/where you do it is unimportant.

During your 'mindful moments', practise tuning into everything you feel, hear and see. For example, when you're cleaning your teeth, listen to the water as it comes out of the tap. Hear the noise your toothbrush makes on your teeth and any other sounds in the room, note the toothpaste's taste and texture in your mouth, etc. Get in touch with how you feel in that moment.

Practising mindfulness every day will encourage your subconscious mind to be present; it will calm the nervous system and help you manage unnecessary automatic worrisome or negative thoughts.

93 - De-Clutter

A cluttered environment can indicate a cluttered mind. Having a good clear out both physically and mentally can open up headspace for more important things.

Start by making a list of everything you need to cleanse, and tackle each one systematically; starting with the potentially most significant impact first. If de-cluttering *everything* seems overwhelming, start small. Each day, choose one thing that you want to clear and get straight into action. Don't give your brain time to talk you out of it (use the 'Five-Second Rule' MM No 22 – Beating Procrastination). You could include:

- Your desk, computer files/emails
- Your car, garage, attic/ loft, kitchen (or 'that drawer' where everything ends up), closet/ wardrobe
- Your friends! (Review your 'friends' list, consider removing/ 'unfollowing' those doom-mongers or toxic people who leave you feeling drained)
- Your unhelpful habits and outdated thinking patterns.

You could even make some money by selling unwanted items or giving them to charity, triggering the release of 'happy hormones' (dopamine, oxytocin and endorphins).

94 – Limit News Exposure

If you're trying to maintain a positive mindset, one of the worst things you can do is have a continuous news stream in the background; especially if you're prone to 'victim' style thinking. *We have to remain consistent with our view of ourselves and the world*, and we look for things to back it up; if you're a negative thinker, the news does that perfectly.

As humans, anticipating the next 'threat' is deeply rooted within our DNA. It is a primal survival need designed to keep us safe. Prolonged exposure to the news, triggers that need and keeps us on false high alert, causing elevated levels of stress. Over the years, there have been numerous research studies on news psychology, and overwhelming evidence shows ONLY BAD NEWS SELLS.

The constant bombardment of negative stories and images we receive through the media can be hugely detrimental to our mental health in the long-term. It's one thing to be aware of what's happening globally; it's something else entirely to be obsessed with it; it's unhealthy and unhelpful. I suggest limiting your exposure to headlines once or twice a day.

95 – Stop Giving Away Your Power

Most people are guilty of giving away their power at some point in their lives; however, some of us have become so accustomed to it, that we don't even realise that we're doing it. When you give away your power, you confirm that your needs are unimportant to yourself and others. You give it away every time you:

• Do something you don't want to do to avoid conflict or stop people thinking badly of you.
• Can't bring yourself to say no, even when you should.
• Fail to set adequate boundaries.
• Neglect to tell someone when they do something you don't like or that upsets you.
• Mind-read, i.e. believing you know what others are thinking or saying about you without any evidence.
• Stop yourself from doing something because of what others may think.
• Put someone else's needs above your own for no good reason (people-pleasing).

If you recognise that you do these types of things, maybe NOW is the time to take your power back. Setting boundaries, and doing things for you is not selfish; it's critical to your overall well-being.

Stop thinking, start doing.

96 - Diarise 'Me' Time

It's critical to schedule time specifically for you. By schedule, I mean put the time in the diary and make it immovable, just as you would any important meeting. Use that time to do something that makes you happy, e.g. yoga, meeting friends, exercising, visiting a coffee shop, reading your favourite book, etc.

Many people struggle with this concept, feeling guilty at the prospect of taking time out for themselves. However, *'you can't pour from an empty cup'*. If you're running on empty, you can't realistically expect to be 100% productive. Therefore, taking time to replenish your mind, body, and soul is a must, NOT a 'nice to have'.

Doing a little of what makes you happy every day is proven to reduce the stress response's effects, triggering happy neurochemicals. You may get some resistance from others at first, especially if they aren't used to you doing things just for you. However, take responsibility; you likely created that scenario; take this as the nudge you need to change.

If you're feeling happier and healthier, not only will it be good for you, but those around you'll also benefit; *behaviour breeds behaviour*.

97 - You Are What You Eat

Food is fuel and what you eat has a massive influence on how you feel, your energy levels, your brain functioning and overall health and well-being. However, a good diet doesn't have to be tedious, time-consuming or expensive. Here are some great tips for eating more healthily:

- Avoid the lure of ready meals by batch cooking. Take some time over the weekend (use N.E.T. time) and put on some great music or a Podcast or have your family do it with you and cook healthy dishes that you can freeze and warm up during the week.

- Look for recipes which are healthy and quick to prepare. Joe Wicks and Jamie Oliver both have cookbooks with meals containing uncomplicated ingredients that are quick and easy to make.

- Plan your meals for the week ahead, that way you're less likely to buy unhealthy ready meals/processed food or order takeaways.

Many of us underestimate the harmful effects of a poor diet, especially the long-term impact; when you change to a more healthy diet, you also boost your immune system and overall ability to fight infection and disease.

98 – Drink More (Water!)

Water is responsible for several vital processes within the body, including removing toxins and waste, maintaining blood circulation, supplying other nutrients to where they're needed, and regulating our internal body temperature.

The brain and heart are composed of approximately 73% water, and the lungs are about 83%. The skin contains around 64% water, muscles and kidneys are 79%, and even the bones are 31% water; this means that dehydration, even as small as 2%, can have a negative effect on the brain and other bodily functions.

Dehydration and a loss of sodium and electrolytes can cause acute memory and attention changes, plus headaches and even migraines.

To prevent any loss of body or brain function, take steps to keep yourself properly hydrated. Women should aim to drink at least 2 litres of water a day, 2.5 litres for men (you'll need more if you're sweating/exercising).

Plain water (still or carbonated) is preferable as added colour or flavour must be processed through the kidneys, whereas 'plain' water flushes straight through.

99 - Act Like a Super Hero!

If you know that you have to do something that you're nervous about, e.g. have a difficult conversation or attend an interview, you can trick your brain into feeling more in control by consciously changing your body language.

Recent research by Amy Cuddy (author of 'Presence') has proven that adopting a 'power stance' (think 'Superman') positively affects our biochemistry. Try it for yourself:

1. Stand up tall and strong with your feet apart. Put your hands on your hips, tighten your stomach muscles, put your shoulders back, push your chest out and lift your chin.

2. Take some long, deep breaths – in through the nose, out through the mouth.

3. Hold the stance for a minimum of two minutes, and you'll release small amounts testosterone and cortisol (ladies, not enough to give you a hairy chest!), which increase performance by making us feel more powerful.

This technique is straightforward and works every time. Use it anytime you need a boost of confidence.

100 – Condition Yourself for Success

One of the many things that the COVID-19 pandemic has taught us is that life is short, and it's not always the big or expensive things that make us happy. Incorporating the following practices into your daily routine will not only make you feel better, but they'll help condition your nervous system for success:

- Laugh more, releasing endorphins.
- Search for the positives in every day, no matter how hard it is (reframe).
- Do something every day that makes you happy – even if it's something small.
- Be kinder to yourself and others – we're all doing our best; *if we knew better, we'd do better.*
- Regularly practise self-care activities; remember, *you can't pour from an empty cup.*
- Practise 'Gratitude' - there is *always* something to be grateful for, being grateful positively affects our well-being and resilience.

Remember, *you can't always choose what happens to you, but you can decide your response*, and finally, *if you always do what you've always done, you'll always get what you've always got!*

Jo Banks

What Next?

Jo Banks

21 Self-Care Tips

The following is a list of twenty-one self-care ideas intended to help increase your resilience and well-being, which are particularly useful if you're feeling less than resourceful.

Taking action, especially when you do something that you don't usually do, is the quickest way to change your mood, get out of a downward spiral and build your positivity. The more you make a habit of doing positive and uplifting things each day (even if it's only for 10-minutes), the happier and healthier you will become. You will be conditioning your nervous system for happiness now rather than at some point in the dim and distant future.

Self-care is not wishy-washy or even 'nice to have'; it's critical to our mental health and well-being. Taking care of our body, mind, and soul is THE most important thing you can do to combat stress, anxiety and depression and bolster your feel-good neurochemicals; dopamine, oxytocin, serotonin and endorphins.

Self-care = Self-worth

In my experience, the amount of self-care someone is

willing to take, directly equates to how much importance they place on their own self-worth. People who see themselves as less important than others tend not to look after themselves, mistakenly believing that it's selfish, they don't have time, or that serving the needs of others is more important. However, as I've said numerous times throughout this book, you can't help others if you're so depleted that you've nothing left to give.

If you feel exhausted, stressed and irritable, your ability to help and support others will severely diminish. The more stressed you get, the more likely it is that you'll end up in a negative downward spiral, repeatedly triggering the stress response and releasing the neurochemicals that can negatively impact your physical and mental health. Therefore, it's critical to take responsibility and care for yourself, not just today, but every day.

21 Self-Care Tips

1. Listen to music that helps you recall happy memories or that makes you feel good. Create a playlist full of uplifting songs that make you feel good and listen to it frequently. If appropriate, sing out loud; it doesn't matter if you can't sing, who cares?! If it makes you feel good, do it, no matter who else is around.

2. Take a brisk 15-minute walk, preferably outside where there's plenty of green, e.g. park, countryside or the beach if you're lucky enough to live near one. Being in nature is incredibly important; not only is it clinically proven to reduce stress, but it also boosts our immune system.

3. Read a chapter of your favourite book – the more inspiring, the better. Self-development books are great for giving us positive ideas. I've listed some of my favourites in the 'Self-Development' chapter of this book. Alternatively, get lost in your favourite novel for a while.

4. Watch a movie that you know will make you laugh – (However, I'm not suggesting 'numbing' here, e.g. Netflix binging!). Laughter changes our biochemistry, releasing endorphins and other feel-good hormones, which again, boost our immune system.

5. Book a massage, pedicure, manicure – or all three if you can afford it. Pampering yourself and taking some time out for personal R&R; equally critical for men and women – you'll also release all four feel-good hormones.

6. Spend five-minutes visualising your perfect day, week, month, year, life(!) in as much detail as possible. Envisioning things how you want them to

be (as if you already have them), will help you feel more optimistic about the future. It will also trigger your Reticular Activating System, moving you towards what you want. Again, it also conditions your nervous system for success. It's a simple but incredibly powerful tool.

7. Do something creative – paint, draw, read, sew, write, jigsaw, woodwork, DIY, etc. When you do these types of activities, you'll be using the creative, right side of your brain, enabling the logical left side to solve any problems you may have in the background.

8. Draw a warm bath with relaxing oils or bubbles. After a good long soak, get into clean PJs *and* clean sheets, have an early night and get some quality, uninterrupted sleep. Aim for a full eight hours.

9. Plan something to look forward to within the next six weeks, e.g. day trip, a spa day, theatre, a day with friends/family, national park, seaside, weekend city break, etc. Having something to look forward to helps the mind focus on something positive and automatically generates happy feelings.

10. Plan a break away within the next six months. It doesn't have to be anything expensive or abroad. Getting out of your typical environment, even for a short time, changing your usual routine, has a

massive positive effect on our well-being.

11. Go to your preferred coffee shop, order your favourite drink and spend a glorious half-hour reading a favourite book or magazine. Alternatively, simply do nothing, but people watch!

12. Buy a large jar with a lid. Write down one good thing that happens every day. When you're feeling less than resourceful, empty the notes and take some time to read all the positive things that you've experienced in the previous weeks or months.

13. Meet up with a good friend or family member who is on the same wavelength and 'gets' you. Spend some quality time with them – try not to complain or gossip – positivity only! Remember, a trouble shared is a trouble halved.

14. Declutter your workspace or an area in your home that is bugging you. Decluttering gives you a sense of achievement (releasing dopamine) and often has the added benefit of clearing your mind, giving you much-needed headspace.

15. Finish an unfinished project or task. It could be something that you are procrastinating about in the house or at work. Schedule and complete it within an achievable timescale. You'll get great satisfaction

from finally removing it from your to-do list. Motion creates more motion, and once you start, it's likely that you'll want to complete other outstanding projects, giving you a real sense of achievement. Use The Five-Second Rule (MM No 22) if you're struggling to get started.

16. Go on a news and social media fast for 48 hours - stop watching/reading the news and turn off your phone alerts. Consciously choose to remove that negativity from your life for at least a couple of days.

17. Meditate for 10-minutes a day, or if you find that difficult, listen to some guided meditation or self-hypnosis. I highly recommend, Andrew Johnson, Paul McKenna and Andrew Sealey for this; I've included their details in the 'Self-Development' chapter later in the book.

18. Take some time to think about your goals for the next 12-months. Get some flip chart paper (I like the sticky A3 Post-it notes) and some felt pens and get creative. When you're happy with what you've got, stick your plans up in a place that you can easily see them every day. They will be a conscious AND subconscious reminder of what you expect to achieve and set your R.A.S. into action.

19. Start a gratitude journal. Use a beautiful book that

you know you'll enjoy writing in. Each morning or evening (or both) start capturing the things for which you're grateful. Endeavour not to repeat the same things, that way; you'll train your brain to look for the positives in each day rather than focusing on the negatives or becoming complacent and simply going through the motions. You might use the 'jar' idea (No 12 above), for this instead of a journal.

20. Move your body, whether that's doing yoga, running, cycling, football, swimming, gym, etc., or ideally, a mixture of activities. When we change our physiology, we change how we feel. Choose something that you enjoy, and you'll be much more likely to stick to it, even if it's just for an hour a week.

21. Make an effort to give a compliment to at least one person every day. It doesn't have to be big, but it has to be genuine and heartfelt. When we compliment others, we release oxytocin. It also starts a ripple effect out into the world. We never know what a difference we can make with one seemingly small gesture that costs us nothing.

Self-Development

Self-development is essential to our growth, and yet, many of us overlook it, mistakenly believing that we don't have time or that's 'not for people like me'. Making a habit of self-development (you could include it in your 'Me Time' - MM No 96) is critical to developing a growth mindset.

If time is an issue, look for occasions where you can multi-task and use N.E.T. (No Extra Time), such as listening to a book or podcast when you're driving or exercising.

Following are some of my favourite books, authors, scientists and self-help specialists who have influenced me most recently (N.B. I am not affiliated with anyone on this list nor do I receive any financial benefits for my recommendations):

Books

- The Five-Second Rule – Mel Robbins
- The Subtle Are of Not Giving a F*ck – Mark Manson
- Can't Hurt Me – David Coggins
- Breaking the Habit – Joe Dispenza
- Greenlights – Matthew McConaughey

- Atomic Habits – James Clear
- Why We Sleep – Matthew Walker
- Sapiens: A Brief History of Humankind - Yuval Noah Harari

Classics include:

- Change Your Life in Seven Days – Paul McKenna
- The Power of Now – Eckhart Tolle
- Awaken the Giant Within – Anthony Robbins
- The Secret – Rhonda Byrne
- The Success Principles - Jack Canfield
- Psycho-Cybernetics – Maxwell Maltz
- The Chimp Paradox – Prof Steve Peters

Podcasts

Podcasts have been a life-saver for me recently. During the second COVID lockdown, I hurt my back and couldn't do any exercise other than walking. To make best use of my walking time and because I'm an avid learner, not only did I listen to audiobooks, but I discovered a new-found love of Podcasts. Here are some of my favourites:

- The Rich Roll Podcast – Rich Roll
- The School of Greatness - Lewis Howes
- The Tim Ferriss Show – Tim Ferriss
- Under the Skin – Russell Brand
- The Joe Rogan Experience – Joe Rogan

They all have such a wide variety of topics and guests that it's hard not to find something enjoyable. Also, I've found that listening to one subject matter expert leads to another. Podcasts are a great way to open yourself up to a whole range of subjects and topics that you may previously never have encountered.

Meditation/ Self-Hypnosis

Meditation and self-hypnosis are another clinically proven method of reducing the effects of stress, anxiety and other mental health issues. It has also shown to be particularly useful in developing a growth mindset and is an integral part of many successful peoples' daily routines.

Pure meditation on its own can be challenging to begin with, as training your mind to stay still and not to wander can take some practice. Therefore, I recommend, at least in the beginning, using guided meditation.

I use a combination of tracks from the following people in my daily practice and highly recommend them (links to their work are in the reference section):

- Paul McKenna – Most of Paul's books come with self-hypnosis/guided meditation elements specifically designed to reinforce learning.
- Andrew Johnson – As well as having downloadable

self-hypnosis and guided meditation tracks on his website, Andrew also has Apps (available in IOS and Android formats) on a whole range of topics including 'Deep Sleep', 'Stress-Free', 'Positivity', 'Lose Weight', to name but a few.

- Michael Sealey – Michael has the most listened to/ watched guided meditation/self-hypnosis videos on YouTube. Each one contains a link to a site where you can purchase and download the track for a nominal fee; by doing that, you avoid the YouTube adverts waking you up at the end of each one.

Training Courses

Learning new skills is a great way to release stress and to keep your brain healthy and active. Life-long learning is again something that most successful people see as a critical factor in achieving exceptional results.

- Download and complete an online course on a topic of interest. I have a range of virtual classes on a range of subjects from 'Building Resilience' to landing 'Your Dream Job'; I also have some free ones available. Visit my online school at www.what-next.teachable.com/courses.
- Sign up for a course at your local college. Many have a wide range of subjects available from academic

topics to hobbies such as ceramics, life-drawing, photography, etc. Many are available in distance learning formats so that you can complete them at your own pace.

- Book a weekend away to learn a new skill, e.g. cooking, yoga, painting, creative writing, etc. There are lots to choose from, and it's also a great way to meet new and interesting people and get you out of your comfort zone.

Jo Banks

Other Stuff!

Jo Banks

References

- Jo's website:
  http://jobanks.net

- Jo's corporate business website, What Next Consultancy (UK) Ltd:
  http://whatnextconsultancy.co.uk

- Jo's online training school:
  https://what-next.teachable.com

- Jo's popular job-hunting book and online career management programme, 'Your Dream Job':
  http://yourdreamjob.co.uk

- Jo's first book, 'Thoughts Become Things':
  http://thoughtsbecomethings.co.uk

- Amy Cuddy 'Presence'
  https://www.amycuddy.com

- Dr Andrew Huberman, Neuroscientist
  http://www.hubermanlab.com

- Dr Jud Brewer, Neuroscientist
  https://drjud.com

- Paul McKenna – Guided meditation/ hypnosis
  https://www.paulmckenna.com

- Michael Sealey – Guided meditation/ hypnosis
  https://www.youtube.com/user/MichaelSealey

- Andrew Johnson – Guided meditation/ hypnosis
  https://www.andrewjohnson.co.uk

- Xmind (mind-mapping tool)
  https://www.xmind.net

- Daily Planner - Best Self Co.
  https://uk.bestself.co

Acknowledgements

Firstly, a huge thank you to my fabulous friends, Sharon Cunningham, Melanie Jones, Michelle Kirby (and the Kirby family, Mark, Emily and Laura), and Justine Williams. I can't imagine my life without you all. You keep me sane, providing copious amounts support (and fizz). I love you guys; I don't think I could do it without you.

Special thanks to my wonderful friends, Basil Zocca and Andy O'Sullivan, for keeping me rational(ish) especially during lockdown. For checking in on me and making sure I'm not going completely bonkers, 'Miss Havisham' stylie, and for our many 'socially-distanced' summer walks.

Gratitude to the gorgeous Wendy Dolan, hairdresser extraordinaire; you keeps me looking presentable (no mean feat) as well as listening to my many and varied woes and for also being a genuinely fabulous friend.

Big thanks to Sean Watts, my 'accountability partner-in-crime', who has allowed me to bounce around my many and varied ideas, insecurities and plans over the last twelve months. For providing me with much-needed feedback and clarity during an incredibly tough year and for keeping me focused and on track.

Jo Banks

Big thanks to my Dad, who's always there for me, regardless of how naughty I am!

Finally, Gratitude goes all of my clients past and present, with special recognition to my 'super clients', Lyndsay Chambers, Jan Norris, Laura Pierce, Debbie Hinbest, Stephen Joyce, Diane Hall, Lizi Ralph, Beth Tohill, Hannah Hadfield and Anna Chenery. Your continued trust and support means more than I can possibly say.

About the Author

Jo Banks, a Business Owner, Transformational Coach, NLP Master Practitioner and CBT Therapist has more than 20 years' experience as a Senior HR Professional, before establishing her Coaching and Consultancy Practice, What Next Consultancy (UK) Ltd in 2009.

Through working within a range of industries, Jo has a strong track record in creating high-performance cultures and dealing with complex people-related issues.

Jo is passionate about helping individuals and organisations to reach their full potential through her proven and innovative coaching style.

While she has trained in traditional coaching methods, she has found her own unique style focusing on creating behavioural change by coaching many hundreds of people; fundamentally changing their thought patterns to achieve tangible results, super-charging their performance, elevating their careers and businesses to the next level.

Jo also runs leadership development training programmes and regularly delivers inspirational speeches on building resilience, emotional intelligence, conflict management, communication skills, effective leadership, etc.

Her work focuses predominantly on challenging thoughts and perceptions, providing a unique blend of information and practical tools and techniques that are easy to use, but create long-lasting behavioural change.

Jo's philosophy is that anyone can change and live a happier, healthier, more productive life, regardless of age, upbringing or current situation. Once people understand their triggers, thoughts and behaviours, they can begin to make a significant difference in their lives with minimal effort.

Visit jobanks.net for more information and to read Jo's popular blog on a wide range of motivational topics. Follow her on social media for the most up to date practical tips, tools, and advice to deal with topical, everyday issues.

Connect with Jo

Instagram:	jobanks247
Twitter:	@JoBanks247
Facebook:	facebook.com/jobanks.net
Web 1:	http://jobanks.net
Web 2:	http://whatnextconsultancy.co.uk
Web 3:	http://yourdreamjob.co.uk
Web 4:	http://thoughtsbecomethings.co.uk
Online training:	https://what-next.teachable.com
Blog:	http://jobanks.net/blog

Jo Banks

Jo Banks

Jo Banks

Jo Banks

Printed in Great Britain
by Amazon